D1546273

PROVIDING CARE for Children of Alcoholics

CLINICAL & RESEARCH PERSPECTIVES

———— Edited By ————

DAVID C. LEWIS, M.D. & CAROL N. WILLIAMS, Ph.D.

A BOOK FROM:

BROWN UNIVERSITY
CENTER FOR ALCOHOL STUDIES

Published by: Health Communications, Inc.
1721 Blount Road, Suite #1
Pompano Beach, FL 33069

About The Brown University Center for Alcohol Studies

Brown has had an active alcohol studies program since 1976. In response to the national need for further alcohol studies, Brown University established the Center for Alcohol Studies in 1982.

The Center for Alcohol Studies seeks to reduce the health risk associated with excessive alcohol use through education and training programs, the application of research findings, and the development of public health policy.

The research program encourages multidisciplinary approaches to the problems related to the use of beverage alcohol. Intervention research is a major interest of the faculty.

The thirty Brown University faculty associated with the Center represent a diverse group with expertise in medicine, psychiatry, community health, psychology and anthropology. The Director of the Center is David C. Lewis, M.D., Professor of Medicine and Community Health.

This book is but one manifestation of the Center's interest in the children of alcoholics. The faculty of the Center are now engaged in several clinical programs providing care for the children of alcoholics. There is also a prevention program and several research projects focused on this population.

5/95

Published by
Health Communications, Inc.
1721 Blount Road, Suite 1
Pompano Beach, Florida 33069

ISBN 0-932194-34-6

Printed in the United States of America

Cover Design by Reta Kaufman

Gift
J.W.

Contents

Contributors iv

About Brown University v

Introduction vi

Chapter One 1
Social and Cultural Factors in Families with
Alcohol-Related Problems
by Dwight B. Heath, Ph.D.

Chapter Two 9
Child Development and Alcoholism: Life-span Implications of
Early Ingestive Behavior and the Drinking Milieu
by Lewis P. Lipsitt, Ph.D.

Chapter Three 19
Fetal Alcohol Syndrome
by John R. Evrard, M.D., M.P.H.

Chapter Four 31
Familial Patterns of Alcoholism
by Migs Woodside

Chapter Five 39
Children of Alcoholic Families
by Michael Liepman, M.D.; William Taylor White, M.S.N.;
and Ted D. Nirenberg, Ph.D.

Chapter Six 65
Clinical Intervention with Children of Alcohol Abusers
by Laura Chakrin Cable, A.C.S.W.; Nora E. Noel, Ph.D.;
and Suzanne C. Swanson, R.N.C., C.A.C.

Chapter Seven 81
Children of Alcoholics: One Experience at Brown
by Bruce E. Donovan, Ph.D.

Chapter Eight 91
The Connection Between Alcoholism, Child Maltreatment,
and Family Disruption
by Carol N. Williams, Ph.D. and Edward W. Collins, M.D.

Chapter Nine 103
Children of Alcoholic Parents: Public Policy Issues
Sheila B. Blume, M.D.

Contributors

Sheila B. Blume, M.D., Medical Director, Alcoholism and Compulsive Gambling Program, South Oaks Hospital, Amityville, New York and Clinical Professor of Psychiatry, State University of New York at Stony Brook.

Laura Chakrin Cable, ACSW, Clinical Social Worker and School Consultant, East Bay Mental Health Center, Barrington, Rhode Island and the Community Counseling Center, Pawtucket Rhode Island.

Edward W. Collins, M.D., Director, Department for Children and Their Families, State of Rhode Island.

Bruce E. Donovan, Ph.D., Associate Dean for Chemical Dependency, Associate Dean of The College, and Professor of Classics, Brown University, Providence, Rhode Island.

John R. Evrard, M.D., Professor of Obstetrics and Gynecology, Brown University, Providence, Rhode Island.

Dwight B. Heath, Ph.D., Professor of Anthropology, and Director, Latin American Studies Center, Brown University, Providence, Rhode Island.

David C. Lewis, M.D., Professor of Medicine and Community Health and Director, Center for Alcohol Studies, Brown University, Providence, Rhode Island.

Michael R. Liepman, M.D., Medical Coordinator, Alcohol Dependence Treatment Program, Veterans Administration Medical Center, and Assistant Professor of Psychiatry and Human Behavior, Brown University, Providence, Rhode Island.

Lewis P. Lipsitt, Ph.D., Professor of Psychology and Medical Science, and Director, Child Study Center, Brown Univeristy, Providence, Rhode Island.

Ted D. Nirenberg, Ph.D., Chief, Alcohol Dependence Treatment Program, Veterans Administration Medical Center, and Assistant Professor of Psychiatry and Human Behavior, Brown University, Providence, Rhode Island.

Nora E. Noel, Ph.D., Co-manager, Butler Evaluation of Treatment of Alcoholism Project, Butler Hospital, and Clinical Assistant Professor in Psychiatry and Human Behavior, Brown University, Providence, Rhode Island.

Suzanne C. Swanson, RNC, CAC, Rhode Island Group Health Association, Providence, Rhode Island.

Carol N. Williams, Ph.D., Assistant Director, Center for Alcohol Studies, Brown University, Providence, Rhode Island.

Migs Woodside, President, Children of Alcoholics Foundation, New York City, New York.

William Taylor White, RN, MSN, CS., Clinical Unit Coordinator of the Addictions Treatment Unit, and Acting Program Director, New Day Center, Fuller Memorial Hospital, South Attleboro, Massachusetts.

Introduction

The impetus for this volume began at a conference about children of alcoholics which was sponsored by the Center for Alcohol Studies and held at Brown University. At that conference it became clear that a book describing the clinical approaches to children of alcoholics but which also incorporated theory, research findings, and policy issues related to treatment was timely and was needed.

There has been an enormous growth of interest in adult and youthful children of alcoholics in the last three years. Treatment and prevention programs are beginning to attend to the needs of this population, estimated to number up to 28 million individuals. National organizations —The Children of Alcoholics Foundation, The National Association for Children of Alcoholics, and the National Foundation for Prevention of Chemical Dependency Disease have been formed and are focusing on different aspects of the problem. The National Institute on Alcohol Abuse and Alcoholism has made research concerning children of alcoholics a priority and has issued an invitation to researchers to submit grant applications for studies of this population.

Genetic and familial studies support the concept that both heredity and environment influence the development of alcoholism. That hereditary factors are not only involved in the intergenerational transmission of alcoholism, but also that heredity may be a major contributing cause of alcoholism, has received the most attention. Researchers have been stimulated to search for biological differences between young children of alcoholics and children of non-alcoholic parents and to pursue the quest for genetic markers of laboratory tests that can identify the risk for the development of alcoholism. Current thinking is that alcoholism is not likely to be tied to a single genetic defect. What may be inherited is the susceptibility to developing alcoholism.

What has also gained a lot of attention has been the identification of developmental problems encountered by children of alcoholics and how the problems experienced by young children are carried into adult life. While it is widely believed that these problems are unique to children of alcoholics, this is not yet certain. Unique or not, understanding the family dynamics in families with an alcoholic parent has enhanced our general understanding of how families interact, how problems develop, and how they are resolved.

The clearest immediate benefit of the attention given to the problems of children of alcoholics has been the relief of guilt for adult children of alcoholics who come to realize that what they took personally about their parents' behavior toward them was not a lack of affection or love, but, in large measure, a manifestation of alcoholism.

The chapters in this volume represent a diversity of viewpoints. The authors were asked to address the topic of children of alcoholics using a critical analysis of the scientific and clinical information available from the vantage point of their own scholarly and clinical experience. The result is a truly multidisciplinary treatment of the topic.

In the first chapter Dwight Heath, an anthropologist, reminds us that our concepts of what constitutes family, and what a family problem or an alcohol problem is, lies in the eyes of the beholder and the culture within which he or she lives. He warns against simplistically assuming that alcohol abuse is always disruptive to families or that children are always harmed by it. Sometimes it can serve as a stabilizing force, and sometimes it helps the children develop positive strengths and characteristics. Dr. Heath asks us to regard the current state of knowledge about children of alcoholics with a grain of salt. Their issues have only just begun to be studied and the focus has been one-sided on the negative effects. We know very little about the children who do not develop problems or whether these dynamics are unique to families with alcoholism or whether they apply to any family facing chronic disease.

Lewis Lipsitt, a developmental psychologist, brings a quarter century of work on infant development and behavior to bear on the issue of drinking behavior. He relates drinking to his studies of self-regulatory behaviors, particularly infant ingestive behavior. Babies have hedonistic pleasure curves by which they try to maximize pleasurable stimuli and minimize annoying ones. How they develop coping skills and regulate their behaviors, especially ingestive ones, over the life span involves an interaction between family, environment, historical circumstances and individual development.

The impact of excessive alcohol use on the physical development of the fetus is the concern of John Evrard, an obstetrician. The immediate effects of a drink on the fetus and the longterm developmental consequences of high alcohol ingestion during pregnancy as well as ways to intervene and prevent these consequences are discussed.

Migs Woodside, who is bringing the needs of children of alcoholics to public attention through her leadership role as President of the Children of Alcoholics Foundation, examines how susceptible children are to inheriting alcoholism. She presents evidence that some forms of alcoholism may have an inherited basis. In a succinct review of the literature, she delineates many of the research questions that still need to be addressed in this fledgling field.

Michael Liepman, William White, and Ted Nirenberg provide a comprehensive overview of the clinical and research literature on children of alcoholics. What is known about risks for addiction, biological differences, impact on developmental tasks of childhood, and family dynamics are covered. Based on their therapy experiences with alcoholic families as a psychiatrist, nurse, and psychologist, respectively, they make recommendations for clinical interventions with these families.

In a continuation of the theme of clinical interventions, Laura Chakrin Cable, Nora Noel, and Suzanne Swanson, a social worker, a psychologist, and a nurse, respectively, discuss the varieties of interventions that can be accomplished with children of alcoholics. Some involve the child directly through individual, group, or family counseling or school alcohol education programs, while others work indirectly with the parents or other family members rather than the child. Important issues of patient treatment matching and evaluation of the effectiveness of these modalities are raised.

Bruce Donovan, a college dean, gives an in-depth description of the implementation of a support group for children of alcoholics on a college campus and vividly describes its evolutionary process, giving pointers such as to what to do and and not do when running such a group. He delineates some of the special issues facing these college age students.

An area that is especially painful to address when discussing children of alcoholics is that of physical and emotional neglect, abuse, and incest. Carol Williams, a social policy analyst, and Edward Collins, a pediatrician, provide an historical context within which to understand the reluctance of society and individuals to intrude into family situations. Practical advice on how to identify and intervene into such situations is offered to clinicians and alcohol counselors.

In the concluding chapter, Sheila Blume, a psychiatrist and alcohol policy analyst, points out that in our desire to help children of alcoholics, we can do harm if we do not pay careful attention to issues such as labeling, confidentiality, parental consent, and individual versus societal rights. Public education and prevention efforts are among the issues she discusses.

The children of alcoholics bring the experiences, biology, and family problems of their young lives into adulthood. The issues that face them at all stages of their lives encompass a broad spectrum of clinical issues and research concerns. This book invites you to a greater awareness of what is known and not yet known about the world of the children of alcoholics.

Brown University Center for Alcohol Studies   David C. Lewis, M.D.
Providence, Rhode Island   Carol N. Williams, Ph.D.

Chapter One
Social and Cultural Factors in Families with Alcohol-Related Problems

Dwight B. Heath, Ph.D.

Throughout human history, the family in its various forms has constituted the primary social unit of all societies. I use the phrase various forms because the monogamous pattern (with only one spouse of each sex) is, in statistical terms, very rare in comparison with polygyny (one male and two or more females), although it is more common that polyandry (one female with two or more males). Regardless of the number of partners involved, marriage—in the most general terms of social recognition of a long-term set of intimate rights and obligations between consenting adults—is the social institution that regulates sexual access. The social recognition of parenthood is often a major determinant in the inheritance of property or other rights, and in succession to various offices and kinds of power. Beyond that, the family (in its parenting aspect) also has primary responsibility for nurturing and socializing children.

In view of the fact that the human infant, when born, is a helpless and ignorant blob of protoplasm, the family is expected to play a crucial role in assuring that such a neonate, without the advantage of several instincts such as many other animals have, can grow up to be a competent member of the society, participating in and contributing to the culture in which it is reared. The process of socialization, as we well know from personal experience, is an ongoing combination of habitual training, partly didactic, partly moral, sometimes by example and other times by exhortation, dealing with techniques, attitudes, values, polity, morality, and a wide range of other human concerns.

In the United States, most people participate in and pay close attention to at least three different kinds of families: the family of orientation (that in which we were reared), the family of procreation (that in which one is a spouse and, at least potentially, a parent), and the affinal family (that assortment of relatives of one's spouse we often call in-laws). The last may sound overwhelmingly large, but that is only because when we think about our own consanguineous relatives (that is, those popularly called blood relatives) we tend to focus on the nuclear family (the conjugal couple and their offspring) and not on the extended family (including married brothers and sisters, uncles, aunts, nephews, nieces, grandparents, and others we might know about in greater or lesser detail, but whom most of us do not think of right away as part of the family).

All of this may sound so simple as to be banal. A social scientist who is on target runs the risk of being dismissed as merely talking common sense, or as dealing with subjects of common knowledge. But that would be an unfair judgment, because what is common sense in one human population may be viewed as weird and even unnatural in another; what is common knowledge right here might well be shocking and difficult to comprehend among people who might live less than five miles from here.

There are several weaknesses in the organization of the nuclear family. Unlike the multigenerational extended family, it lacks built-in babysitters and experienced elders, and for several years, a number of relatively unproductive dependents are supported by only one or two workers. Yet this organization is involved in some of the most difficult and exacting jobs that any organization has: health maintenance, education, and moral inculcation, among others. Families do this 24 hours a day, seven days a week, year after year. It is not surprising that even the most finely tuned of healthy families is subject to stresses and strains.

What is a problem family anyway? This is not a frivolous question: various populations have different attitudes about drinking and its outcomes. Within a single city, there is an enormous variation in what people view as problematic. One informant was distressed about the dangers of her husband's drinking because he once -without even being drunk —unwittingly insulted his boss by mentioning an unprofitable transaction at a party where everyone present already knew the story. A wife complained that her husband spent too much money on drinking, too often came home late, and had lost several jobs because of fighting or absenteeism, both of which can follow heavy drinking. Nevertheless, she was proud that "There really isn't any problem with (Tony)'s drinking; he never hits me the way alcoholics beat their wives." Another household was so concerned about maintaining the cherished image of a long-suffering and abstemious mother that several children between the ages of 6 and 18 all worked at housekeeping and at the conspiratorial fiction that their parents had gone on vacation, even though the mother was quietly drunk in her room for weeks, and even after the father had moved away.

Despite a litany of complaints, another informant excused her husband by boasting that, "At least he never had no trouble with the cops." Another informant had many run-ins with the police during binges, but, "Ain't got no drinking problem; they didn't never put me in jail." And one who has, in fact, spent nearly half of his adult life in jail for various offenses, mostly committed while drunk, takes pride in his supposed self-control: "At least I never killed nobody."

It should be evident that problems, like beauty, are in the eye of the beholder! Insofar as there may be a moral to this, it is that if we hope to be at all effective in changing behavior and helping people, we must pay attention to how those people define problems. By the same token, we should not expect much cooperation if we focus on things that we consider problematic, but that the actors themselves do not view in the same way. A vivid illustration of this is the southwestern Indian who clearly and simply asserts that it would be immoral if he did not get drunk with his buddies at every pow-wow, and whose wife and children are among the many who agree.

In preparing this chapter, I have reread much of what has been written about the impact of alcohol on the family. I must confess to being confused about what some of the authors are trying to get at. There is often an introductory reminder to the effect that "alcoholism runs in families." That seems like an incontrovertible and important point, until one reflects briefly on the fact that speaking German runs in families, as does eating with chopsticks, going to Mass on Sunday, graduating from Yale, being a bank president or a trapeze artist, left-handedness, reading the New Yorker, and a host of other patterns. Please understand that I do not for a moment mean to dismiss the strong and increasing evidence that has come to light, some of it effectively summarized in other chapters in this book, tracing parent-child linkages after adoption, sometimes even with twins. There is a statistically significant probability that there may be some hereditary predisposing factor in some kinds of alcoholism. But that is very different from genetic etiology, and both of those are very different from saying that something "runs in families."

Another weakness of much of the extant literature on the subject is the predominance of a long and dreary chronicle, sometimes relieved by an occasional weak joke, about the difficulties that are suffered by members of a family where one or more of the parents drinks too much. Such information can be important, and it helps people know how children are hurt if they undergo emotional deprivation, confused and confusing signals about what is expected of them, or other kinds of abuse or neglect. But this emphasis is not on hereditary but on environment, not on nature but on nurture, not on the stuff of genetics but on that of the social sciences. Many authors seem to change their tune early in such anecdotal accounts.

Other authors in this book offer more authoritative data on some of the detailed impacts that alcohol can have within a family. What I can most effectively offer as a social scientist is a perspective that deals with the family as a system, and that helps slough off some of the common-sense preconceptions that we share as well-social-ized members of our culture.

A multidisciplinary team at George Washington University has spent several years observing workaday behavior in families in which the parents drink heavily. Their conclusions may surprise some, flying in the face of the predominant theme of so much that is said and written about children of alcoholics. "The manner in which families handle the alcohol abuse behavior has repercus-sions for intergenerational transmission of alcoholism . . . When it is part of the family system, alcohol abuse may actually have stabilizing, rather than disruptive, effect on family interaction in that it can produce highly predictable patterns of interaction that diminish uncertainties about the family's internal life and its rela-tionship to the outside world" (1).

The value of such "highly predictable patterns" seems crucial. When family rituals are adhered to, the children rarely become alcoholics or marry alcoholics; when family rituals are altered in order to accommodate disruptive drunken comportment, the children become alcoholics to a statistically significant degree, and the daughters marry alcoholics in significant numbers.

The quality of social interaction does not always vary in direct proportion to the quantity of alcohol ingested. Much of my research over the years has dealt with Indian tribes in various countries. Many of those who drink the most and are most often deeply intoxicated, appear to have virtually no alcohol-related problems (in economic, social-relational, psychological, or other terms). One need not pick small and exotic culture to illustrate this point, either; Finland has about the lowest per-capita consumption of alcoholic beverages in Europe but is reported to have one of the highest rates of overall alcohol-related problems, whereas France, Italy, and Spain, all with excpeitonally high rates of consumption, all have relatively lower rates of occurrence of various alcohol-related problems.

If consumption figures do not provide a golden key for spotting problems, there may be an inherent weakness to the increasingly popular view that reducing consumption, by raising taxes, indexing the price of drinks, shortening hours of sale, and similar restrictive measures, is the most effective way to diminish alcohol-related problems. By contrast, I submit, it is patterns of belief and behavior that are fundamental if we are to change drinking and its outcomes. Whatever else it may be, drinking is primarily a social act; similarly, whatever else it may be, the family is a social system with a culture of its own.

Whenever we talk about alcoholism (or problem drinking, or alcohol abuse, or the alcohol-troubled person, or alcohol-related problems) we are talking about phenomena that have importance primarily because they involve more than one person, they are social phenomena. Furthermore, these phenomena are important primarily because they do not fit well with any number of cultural beliefs and values; that is to say they are also cultural phenomena. For these reasons, it is crucial to consider such problems as they relate to a number of familiar but important things in our shared experience. For example:

Domineering mothers make for certain kinds of social stresses. An ascetic morality often denies young people access to pleasures that their friends take for granted.

Irregular working hours, or high risks at work, take their toll on workers during their time at home as well as on the job.

These and many more cultural factors occur with different relative frequencies in different segments of a pluralistic society. It also seems likely that each of them is associated with different kinds of stress within and among various members of a family system. Similarly, attitudes are cultural factors that affect interpersonal relations within even a small and generally healthy family system. Illustrative are:

Preoccupation with cleanliness, or the imperative always to excel, can have a telling impact on a child's self-concept.

Eating as an accepted way to find solace shapes one's actions as well as one's body.

The view that "children should be seen but not heard" structures intergenerational communication in potentially disruptive ways.

All of these attitudes occur with different frequency among different populations, and again, it takes little reflection on experience, one's own and that of others, to recognize how intimately they are linked with the potential or the reality of conflict.

These are only a few illustrative examples of social and cultural factors that affect alcohol use and its outcomes. They also prompt us to remember that a belief or behavior that poses problems for one member of a family may very likely serve valuable positive functions for another. Similarly, what is functional for the family as a system may have some limiting or even harmful effects on a given member of the family. Such effects, whether positive or negative, are not necessarily deliberate or consciously planned; they can often result unexpectedly from the internal dynamics of the system, because a family is essentially a network of interrelated statuses and roles.

A key question that seems rarely to be addressed is this: How do the dysfunctional aspects of alcohol-troubled families differ from those of families that are suffering other kinds of crisis? In so complex and finely tuned a social system, morale depends in large part on the delicate interplay of the members in terms of their expected roles. It is for this reason that a systems approach is so important. The family should not be viewed as a machine where trouble in one part may stop or shatter the whole thing, but as a network or web, where strain on any member is partially transmitted to others, usually imposing the need for at least minor adjustments on their part. Too much of such strain can, of course, rupture the family, just as it would a net. But more often the quantity and the direction of strains may shift, sometimes very abruptly, in ways that reshape the linkages, sometimes even returning to a state that looks very much like what it was in the beginning.

Maybe that is what we all should hope for in the case of families that are racked with alcohol-related problems. If so, that is why it is of fundamental importance to learn what people expect their families to do. This is another way of saying that we must learn what roles each person is expected to play. To understand what it means to be a good wife, a good husband, a good son, or a good daughter, is to understand the social organization of a given population. Such meanings differ from one group to another, so it is no mere academic exercise, but a fundamental aspect of understanding people and the nature of their problems.

References

1. Wolin, S.J., Bennett, L.A., Noonan, D.L., and Teitelbaum, M.A. Disrupted family rituals: A factor in the intergenerational transmission of alcoholism. *Journal of Studies on Alcohol,* 1980; 41 (3):199-214.

Chapter Two
Child Development and Alcoholism: Life-span Implications of Early Ingestive Behavior and the Drinking Milieu

Lewis P. Lipsitt, Ph.D.

I cannot overlook the opportunity presented through this forum to express a point of view that may at first seem capricious. The view makes good sense to me, for it is based upon the precepts of behavioral science, particularly developmental psychology, and is strongly supported by years of experience which our culture has now had with the onset and "control" of alcohol ingestion.

Nonetheless, the viewpoint might strike some as odd and perhaps even counter-productive. The suggestion I shall make is contrary to the prevailing point of view that over-ingestion of alcohol, and the problems that individuals have with or as a consequence of alcohol ingestion, are fundamentally matters of disease. Rather, alcohol ingestion is a matter of individual behavior, and is greatly influenced by environmental opportunities and permissions, including societally endorsed incentives (or disincentives) for drinking.

This is not to deny that alcohol intake can lead to disease, such as liver dysfunction. The view, simply, is that in this respect excessive alcohol ingestion is rather like dangerous driving or the propensity that some people have for physical combativeness; it can lead to injury and, indeed, death, but in its origins it must be regarded as *behavioral* misadventure.

The implications of this point of view are that in order to understand completely the onset and perpetuation of debilitating drinking behavior, one must study such questions as the incentive conditions under which the dangerous drinking behavior got started in the first place, the role of familial factors in endorsing or constraining such behavior, the relationship of peer pressures and of life circumstances to drinking patterns, the effects of early experiences of all sorts in setting the conditions for one's drinking patterns, and the influence of special life events (like the loss of a loved one, or encountering a psychotherapeutic opportunity) in promoting or constraining further excessive drinking behavior. In short, the view is taken here that drinking behavior is developmental, and that a life-span developmental orientation must be taken to its study, to include age-related, contextual, and historical conditions. The development of individuals is profoundly affected by all of these. (1,2)

The Notion of Behavioral Control

Control is a behavioral matter, whether we are speaking of "self-control" or of constraints on an individual's actions imposed by society. The latter may include family, peers, or groups with a common point of view or concerted effort to move one's behavior in a particular direction.

The control of behavior is largely a matter of incentives, whether external, internal, or combinations of both. People behave in ways that tend to yield rewards. An example is working to earn food to sustain nourishment and pleasure. Achievement in this task reduces the discomforts of hunger and, in humans, often yields feelings of pride and success and, when the activity produces rewards for others to whom we are close and for whom we have "responsibility," of nurturance. These are all rewards or "response consequences." There is some measure of pleasure involved in all of them.

Incentive-controlled behaviors are largely matters of enhancing pleasure and avoiding annoyance. It is a primordial truth that people, like other organisms controlled by incentives which are available for behaving in certain ways, follow the pleasures of sensation, broadly conceived to include satisfactions relating to the self-concept (3,4,5,6). These are often referred to as hedonic factors, to include both the pleasure and annoyances of sensation.

The Hedonic Control of Behavior: Relation to Alcoholism

Pleasure and displeasure (the latter to include pain and milder annoyances), and the anticipation and discomfort, control the approach and avoidance behavior of all animals, including humans (7,8). The comings and the goings, the doings and the not-doings, of human action are thus under hedonic control. This is not to deny that humans can be altruistic; humans do sometimes give up their pleasures to maximize the pleasures of others, and they even take pleasure in doing so! Humans even elect to endure severe punishments, as is often the case in war and other hazardous conditions in which humans engage themselves, in order to serve or save others. Indeed, attachment to others or to principles often carries the explicit or implicit burden of eventual sacrifice to promote another's pleasure or preserve another's life. It must be understood, therefore, that the "hedonic control" of behavior often entails a ranking and trading of incentive conditions, some of which are social (especially in sentient beings), and sometimes the actual unpleasantness or pleasurable consequences of a given behavior may not be immediately obvious.

Alcohol and Pleasure

If Margaret Mead did not first observe it, I at least learned first from her that civilization probably can be dated from the moment of the first fermentation of fruit. Communal, ritualistic, and recreational drinking of alcoholic beverages has been around since the earliest recorded history of mankind. We do not need to discuss at this time whether our entry into civilization was, in fact, facilitated by the discovery of alcohol or the revelation of delight in drinking. However, this is not a totally unthinkable prospect. We do know that many great works of art and science were conceived under the influence of alcohol, and that exceptional expressions of kindness and even loving moments in personal relationships often have been accompanied by the ingestion of alcohol.

Alcohol use is a virtually universal condition of homo sapiens; there are few cultures known that do not have some form of fermented (and thus, in principle, mind-altering) beverage available for use under conditions sanctioned by the mores of the culture. To be sure, there are some segments of virtually every culture that do not use alcohol, and there are some individuals within alcohol-using cultures that do not ingest the beverage. Typically, the conditions which create the abstention in these instances involve admonitions to individuals that drinking will create havoc in the lives of those who imbibe. This is an example of socially induced anticipation of the possible negatively hedonic consequences of one's behavior, and persons subjected to this type of training may never, ever, drink alcoholic beverages. Another class of abstentive behavior involves individuals who have ingested such beverages in the past and have "sworn off" as a consequence of some unpleasant, annoying, or painful condition that followed. Thus, incentive control is frequently in evidence during abstentive behavior, just as it is during ingestive behavior.

Pleasure and the Milieu

Alcohol is a mind-altering chemical that humans clearly like to consume. Like so many other potentially hazardous conditions of life, including the lead in our air, the pesticides in our food, and warfare, the perils of alcohol ingestion commingle with the verity that alcohol also promotes pleasure. The lead is in our air because there are incentives for traveling faster, more comfortably and, presumably, otherwise more pleasurably that we could by horse and buggy. The pesticides are in our food so that time and funds spent growing crops would yield larger and presumably tastier crops, making us happier. The incentives for warfare, however disagreeable such behavior is in so many respects, are so obvious as to need no elaboration.

Drinking as Behavior

Ingestion is a natural biological act. The impetus for ingestion, from fetal life onward, is the pleasure associated with it. For those reasons, the behavior of drinking is not going to go away. Styles of ingestion are culturally conditioned, and we learn about what is available and how to obtain it from the earliest moments of life. Alcohol, through a nipple or soaked on a sucking cloth, is often used as a pacifier for infants during otherwise unanesthetized circumcisions. Moreover, a sugar solution, for "fussy babies," has been sold over the counter in British pharmacies for decades, and now is available similarly in Canada. It is called "Gripe Water", and it is spiked with alcohol! The dulling of the nervous system's receptivity has always been marketable, particularly as an antidote for pain or annoyance. Alcohol ingestion is a convenient means to this end or, apparently anyway, many societies and millions of people have found it to be so.

The remainder of my remarks will be about behavioral self-regulation in the infant, and the relevance of this for subsequent learning and unlearning of "alcohol-ingesting behavior."

The Relevance of Infantile Behavior

Studying infant behavior and development for over 25 years, I have become impressed with the amazing maturity of the normal, full-term newborn. Previous impressions of the neonate as an unresponsive, virtually helpless creature, with it sensory systems functioning only sluggishly and its nervous system little advanced beyond that of a sub-cortical preparation, are clearly incorrect. (5,7,9). I recall a nurse saying to me a mere two decades ago, while she watched as I moved a red object back and forth across what I thought was the visual field of a four-day-older, "What are you doing that for? Don't you know babies can't see?" When I replied, "Yes, they do, many of them. And they smell, too," she laughed heartily.

In the last 25 years, it has been well demonstrated that normal, full-term infants arrive in the world with all of their sensory systems functioning, and even with the capacity for learning. They are capable with the first few days of life of Pavlovian conditioning, whereby a previously neutral stimulus becomes an effective stimulus through association with a stimulus that already has the capacity to evoke a response. Pavlov paired a metronome sound with a touch of food flavoring to the tongues of dogs and found that the sound would subsequently cause the dogs to salivate. Newborns are like that. They can also learn to repetitively execute a motor response already in their behavioral repertoire, such as head turning, to produce a consistently available response-consequent (reward, or reinforcement). They can learn adaptive "approach behaviors," like turning their heads in the appropriate direction whether the mother puts the child to her left or right breast, and they can learn to engage in behaviors that will diminish the intensity of, or cause "avoidance" of, noxious stimulation.

These observations have led us to believe that behavior from very early in life is under the control of psychobiologically based incentive conditions. Even newborns will act, within their response limits, to maximize the pleasures of sensation and minimize annoying stimulation. When in the natural course of events, as in feeding at the breast, young infants succeed through some behavioral maneuver to accomplish this, they will tend to repeat the gesture if again given the opportunity.

Thus infants capitalize upon their inbuilt reflexes, such as the rooting response (turning the head in the direction of a touch near the mouth), by learning to minimize the delay between such a touch and the eventual connection with the nipple. Similarly, if an infant experiences annoyance while feeding, as can happen if the feeder occludes its nostrils when its mouth forms a tight pressure seal around the nipple, the infant will on future occasions react negatively (read "angrily") to being placed again in a similar position to that which on last occasion resulted in rage.

Newborns come into the world as able individuals, by which one means that they have both approach and avoidance responses. These are based upon the hedonic character (the pleasantness or unpleasantness) of the stimulation available in the environment. In the beginning infants will withdraw from hurtful stimulation (hurt usually being associated with tissue damage and thus threat to life) such as a pinch on the toe or an overly loud sound. They will move toward stimuli that are pleasant, such as the smell of mother's milk, or a touch on the cheek; these stimuli promote warmth and nourishment, and hence survival. Of course, these behaviors are significantly compromised in infants born at risk, and inadequate self-defensive or self-regulatory behaviors may in fact hasten the demise of an infant beset at birth by hazardous biological conditions (10).

The Primacy of Oral Stimulation and of Taste

Newborns have an affinity for the sweet taste (5,6,11). We know that because they behave differently, and their faces even look differently, when they are offered in response to their sucking behavior a solution that is sweet. This is so even if the drops of fluid which they obtain for each suck are a precious .02 milliliter, or about one-sixth the size of the drip that comes from an eye-dropper. If you switch the baby among several different items on the menu, as we do in our neonate laboratory under well controlled conditions with polygraphic monitoring and computer tabulation of behavior, the infant modulates its own behavior to accord with the sweetness of the fluid of which he or she is working.

With increasing sweetness of the fluid, the normal newborn slows down its sucking behavior within bursts of sucking and takes fewer and shorter rest periods or inter-burst intervals (7). Although sucking occurs more slowly for the sweeter fluid (e.g., 15% sucrose as opposed to 5% sucrose, or plain distilled water), the overall number of sucks invested per larger unit of time such as two minutes is larger because of the foreshortened rest intervals. Of great interest is that, regardless of the fact the sucking occurs more slowly within bursts for the sweeter fluids, the infant's heart rate goes to higher levels within those "sweet" bursts, even when we control for length of burst by measuring heart rate on only the first ten sucks of a burst.

All of this suggests that the slower sucking rates for the sweeter fluids represent a sort of savoring event in which the baby enhances the pleasures of sensation by sucking slowly, but signals its enjoyment of the sweet fluid through the enhanced heart rate mediated, as we suppose, by the autonomic nervous system.

It is possible in this way to document for individual infants the extent to which they are "turned on" by the sweeter fluids. Our computer provides a best-fit function for each child, whereupon we are able to gauge that infant's "hedonic slopes" in relation to normative slopes for other infants of the same age and birth condition.

In one study, we were able to show that infants who are born prematurely and small have flatter hedonic slopes (12). Such infants are turned on to a lesser extent by the sweeter fluids, and they continue to show compromised behavior in this respect even when tested at 40 weeks conceptional age, the age of their normal full-term control peers. It appears, therefore, that among their other problems babies born at risk have behavioral deficiencies relating to the experiencing of the pleasures of sensation.

Taking the entire package of findings together, and putting a perhaps too succinct interpretation on all of it, it appears that one of the most salient psychobiological features of human infancy is the capacity to experience the pleasures of sensation, and to engage in self-regulatory behavior. The environment presents the rewarding opportunities and sets the limits for individual behavioral control, but these opportunities enter into a transaction with the infant whereby the baby can at once manifest its tastes and distastes, and learn the "rules" for optimizing the pleasures of sensation and minimizing displeasure or annoyance. In some very important ways, relating to the psychobiological self-regulation of hedonic inputs, infantile behavior bears many similarities to the admittedly more complex self-regulating mechanisms of adulthood. It is a matter largely of speculation at this stage of developmental knowledge, however, just what the consequences are of early experience in effective self-regulation and what are the relative roles ultimately of early and later experience in such adaptations (9). Rutter has suggested on the basis of a survey of relevant studies, however, that human resilience in the presence of stress in later life, may well be attributed in part to mechanisms of endurance and self-reward that have been taken from earlier life experiences.

Defending Oneself: The Experience of Annoyance

Our data indicate that those infants who are less responsive to the sweet taste tend also to be deficient in their other hedonically mediated behaviors. For example, they are less defensive in their responses to annoying stimulation, such as the threat of respiratory occlusion. Newborns who are less reactive in hedonic situations may be at greater risk in later stages of development as well. Crib death may be understood one day as a failure of the infant's self-regulatory system to operate effectively in the presence of ordinarily annoying stimuli (9). Babies born at risk and living under duress, such as those typically found in a neonatal intensive care unit, are often noted to be under-responsive in a number of ways. Their hedonically mediated behavior seems especially deficient; they do not suck well, and they do not often cry, even when subjected to ordinarily painful stimulation. The impression that observers frequently have is that babies in intensive care units, even those not subjected to dulling effects of drugs, often do not seem to "care."

As the pleasures of sensation are often used as antidotes for the expressed annoyance of infants (and in aging humans as well), one must consider the possibility that early life conditions are essentially training grounds in which coping responses can be acquired and which may have lasting significance. Approach-avoidance conflicts and the mechanisms which humans learn for their resolution, are laid down early in development. Suffice it to remind ourselves that many hurtful occasions are followed by satisfying states of affairs. Mothers give their babies a sweet tasting fluid, even spiked with alcohol, when the infant is fussy; children get ice cream when sick in bed with a cold; and the dentist hands out something nice for enduring tooth annoyances. Pacification processes appropriated by parents of fidgety children usually entail conditions of pleasure.

Concluding Comment

Current knowledge concerning the hedonic mediation of behavior in human infants has been reviewed briefly, to suggest that:

1. some of the earliest manifestions of psychobiological self-regulation can serve as a beginning model of self-controlling behavior in adults;

2. human behavior is controlled in large part by the pleasures and annoyance of sensation;

3. ingestive behavior may be particularly subject to determinative influences of the transactions of the person with permissions provided and constraints imposed by the environment;

4. human ingestion of, and particularly excessive use of, alcoholic beverages may be seen as a problem of self-regulatory behavior; and

5. research on alcoholism and its amelioration might be better informed by a life-span approach which assumes that over-ingestion is a problem principally of behavior control, with influences from a variety of sources including age, the social familial context in which the behavior is acquired and perpetuated, and the historical and life-event circumstances in which the drinking takes place.

References

1. Baltes,P.B., Reese, H.W., & Lipsitt, L.P.Life-span developmental psychology. *Annual Review of Psychology*:1980, Vol. 31, pp. 65-110.
2. Garmezy, N. Stressors of childhood. In: N. Garmezy & M. Rutter (Eds) *Stress, Coping, and Development in Children:* 1983, New York, McGraw-Hill.
3. Allen, A.H.B. *Pleasure and Instinct: A Study in the Psychology of Human Action.* New York: Harcourt, Brace, 1930.
4. Beebe-Center, J.G.: *The Psychology of Pleasantness and Unpleasantness.* New York: D. Van Nostrand, 1932.
5. Lipsitt, L.P. The pleasures and annoyances of infants: Approach and avoidance behavior. In: E. Thoman (Ed.), *Origins of the Infant's Social Responsiveness.* The Johnson & Johnson Baby Products Co., Pediatric Round Table II. Hillsdale, NJ: Erlbaum, 1979.
6. Lipsitt, L.P. The pleasures and annoyances of babies: Causes and consequences. In: J.D. Call, E. Galenson, & R.L. Tyson (Eds.), *Frontiers of Infant Psychiatry.* 1984, Vol. II, New York. Basic Books.
7. Lipsitt, L.P.The study of sensory and learning processes of the newborn. In: J. Volpe (Ed.), *Clinics in Perinatology,* 1977, Vol. 4, No. 1, Philadelphia: W.B. Saunders.
8. Rovee-Collier, C. & Lipsitt, L.P. Learning, adaptation, and memory in the newborn. In: P. Stratton (Ed.), *Psychobiology of the Human Newborn.* London, Wiley, 1982.
9. Lipsitt, L.P. Stress in infancy: Toward understanding the origins of coping behavior. In N. Garmezy & M. Rutter (Eds.), *Stress, Coping, and Development in Children.* New York: McGraw-Hill, 1983, pp. 161-190.
10. Lipsitt, L.P. Developmental jeopardy in the first year of life: Behavioral considerations. In A. Baum & J.E. Singer (Eds.), *Handbook of Psychology and Health (Vol. II): Children and Health.* Hillsdale, NJ: Erlbaum, 1982.
11. Steiner, J.E. Human facial expressions in response to taste and smell stimulation. In H.W. Reese & L.P. Lipsitt (Eds.), *Advances in Child Development and Behavior (Vol. 13),* New York: Academic Press 1979, pp. 257-295.
12. Cowett, R.M., Lipsitt, L.P., Vohr, B., & Oh, W. Aberrations in sucking behavior in the low birth weight infant. *Developmental Medicine and Child Neurology,* 1978, 20-701-709.
13. Rutter, M. Stress, coping, and development: Some issues and some questions. In N. Garmezy & M. Rutter (Eds.), *Stress, Coping, and Development in children.* New York: McGraw-Hill, 1983.

Chapter Three
Fetal Alcohol Syndrome

John R. Evrard, M.D., M.P.H.

Many of us are alcoholics, were alcoholics, have a close relative or a friend who is an alcoholic, or are interested in helping alcoholics. We, therefore, know that there is nothing humorous about alcoholism. Nevertheless, numerous jokes about the town drunk are ever with us.

I have considered this phenomenon and have concluded that alcoholic jokes are a mechanism of denial—"the not me syndrome"—and they represent a light manner by which the fine line between social drinking and alcoholism is blurred. A few years ago, four 5-year-old children in France were found to be alcoholics and suffering delirium tremens. In an effort to decrease drinking, the French government posted signs in bars that said, "Alcohol kills slowly." One of the local patrons penciled underneath, "We don't care, we're not in a hurry".

At the Women and Infants Hospital of Rhode Island Ambulatory Unit, we manage about 1,450 prenatal patients a year. On the intake interview, a careful history regarding alcohol ingestion is obtained. An effective method of quantifying alcohol intake is through our nutritionists. Because alcohol is a source of calories, the nutritionists can, in a non—threatening manner, assess the amount of intake. The ambulatory care personnel all try to be as supportive as possible of the pregnant alcoholic. Since most women are concerned about the health of their fetus, more than they are about their own, pregnancy offers a potent motivating force for the women to cut down on their alcohol intake. Recently, one of our nurse practitioners, who, on the patient's first visit had stressed the importance of reducing alcohol intake during pregnancy, saw one of her patients for her next prenatal visit. The patient happily announced that she had switched from Four Roses to Sombreros—because the milk was good for her baby. Denial! Successes are hard to come by when treating pregnant alcoholics, but the results are truly worth the frustration and effort.

The effect of alcohol on the fetus had been suspected for a long time. (In Carthage, the bridal couple was forbidden to drink wine on their wedding night in order that defective children might not be conceived.) It is now recognized that fetal alcohol syndrome is mostly related to heavy drinking. However, the safe quantity of alcohol for use in pregnancy has not been determined. One of the problems associated with research and alcohol is that the professionals studying the problem quantify heavy drinking differently. Consequently, data between studies are difficult to compare. For example, Rosett et al. have defined heavy drinking as consumption of five or six drinks on some occasions and at least 45 drinks per month (1). Russell and Bigler define heavy drinking as drinking three times or more daily regardless of the quantity, or drinking two to three times per month, but taking more than five drinks half of the time (2).

They also have defined an absolute alcohol index. The index defined heavy drinkers as consuming one or more ounces of alcohol per day. This would be equivalent to two cocktails, two cans of beer, or two glasses of wine. Ouellette et al. divided drinkers into three classes. Group one drinkers were abstainers or light drinkers, defined as drinking less than once per month. Group three drinkers averaged 45 ml of absolute alcohol per day. Group two were moderate drinkers and fell in between the two previous categories (3).

Prevalence

It has been estimated by Russell and Bigler that 8% of the women between ages 30 and 39 years of age are problem drinkers. In the past decade, an increasing proportion of women are postponing childbearing until age 30 or after. The prevalence of fetal alcohol syndrome varies with the population being defined, but has been judged to be somewhere just between 1 in 600 to 1 in 1,500 live births (1). At the Boston City Hospital Prenatal Clinic, 9% of the patients were identified as problem drinkers (4). In this study, Rosett et al. followed a population of 332 women. Of these, 13% were heavy drinkers, consuming an average of 5.8 ounces of absolute alcohol per day. Forty percent were moderate drinkers, and 47% were rare drinkers. Their study showed that the heavy drinkers were older and fewer were married or living with the father of the child.

Ethanol Effect on Fetus

Several mechanisms have been postulated for the destructive effect of alcohol on the fetus. Malnutrition seems to be an unlikely cause of the problem. Both the toxic effects of the ethanol and the toxic effects of its breakdown products, such as acetaldehyde, are considered to be major etiologic factors in the production of fetal alcohol syndrome. In the metabolism of ethanol the first oxidative step is catalyzed by alcohol dehydrogenase and nicotinamide adenine dinucleotide. Waltman and Iniquez have demonstrated that in humans alcohol traverses the placenta within one minute. The half life on ethanol in maternal venous blood is between one and four hours. Mothers were given intravenous ethanol shortly before delivery, and the researchers found that the serum alcohol levels in the fetus were equal to or lower than those of the mothers in 22 of 23 patients. However, because the fetus and newborn are deficient in alcohol dehydrogenase, higher levels of ethanol persisted in the newborn longer than in the mother (5).

Effect of Disulfiram on the Fetus

Disulfiram blocks oxidation of the alcohol at the acetaldehyde stage. During alcohol metabolism after disulfiram ingestion, acetaldehyde levels are five to ten times higher than if disulfiram were not taken. Theoretically, therefore, if acetaldehyde is the culprit in the production of fetal alcohol syndrome, the use of disulfiram would be contraindicated during pregnancy. Clinical data support this hypothesis. Favre-Tissot and Delatour, reporting on eight infants born of mothers who were taking disulfiram during pregnancy, found that four had congenital defects not resembling those of fetal alcohol syndrome (6). In another study on five women who were taking disulfiram, there was one spontaneous abortion, two infants born with club feet, and two apparently normal babies. Nora et al. reported on two mothers who were on disulfiram during the first trimester of pregnancy. Both had infants born with limb anomalies (7).

Fetal Alcohol Syndrome

There is a constellation of abnormalities associated with fetal alcohol syndrome. These may be broken down into four major categories of abnormalities (8):
1. growth and development;
2. cranial facial disorders;
3. limb disorders;
4. other disorders such as cardiac abnormalities;
   genital abnormalities;
   ear abnormalities; or
   hemangiomas.

In Fig. 1., Ouellette et al. demonstrate the rate of prematurity, postmaturity, and babies which were born of small gestational age to alcoholics (3). As you recall, group one were abstainers or light

FIGURE I

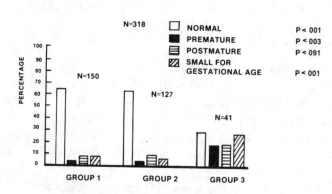

Frequency of Growth Abnormalities in Newborn Infants.
Infants of women who were heavy drinkers were smaller and the risk of prematurity was increased.

Reprinted with permission of the NEW ENGLAND JOURNAL OF MEDICINE, 297:528-530, September 1977.

drinkers, and group three were heavy drinkers. Contrast, therefore, the premature rate in light drinkers of 4% compared to 20% for heavy drinkers, postmaturity 7% for light drinkers compared to 21% for heavy drinkers, and small for gestational age infants, 9% for light drinkers compared to 28% for heavy drinkers. The work of Hanson et al. (Fig. 2) further emphasizes the influence of alcohol on growth (9). They broke down the effect into four categories. Regarding prenatal growth deficiency, 38 of 39 babies exhibited growth deficiency, or 97%. Second, they found that postnatal growth deficiency was present in 37 of 38 infants, or 98%. Microcephaly occurred in 38 of 41 infants (93%) and developmental delay or mental deficiency occurred in 31 of 35 infants (89%). Rosett et al. (1) observed that in women who are heavy drinkers, 45% of the infants were below the 10th percentile weight for their group.

Microcephaly (small head), and retardation are another story and require further discussion. It is a well-known fact that the brain growth spurt begins in the middle of gestation. By then, the adult number of neurons have already been achieved. Only the late dividing granular neurons of the cerebellum could be influenced by late malnutrition. This might result in consequences for motor development, the "clumsy child", if you will. Brandt has demonstrated that between 33½ and 36½ weeks there is a very rapid brain growth of between 121 and 124 gms (10).

The fact that brain developmental problems associated with maternal alcohol intake may cause microcephaly has been confirmed by Jones and Smith (11). Clarren and Smith also pointed out that 85% of the 128 patients had infants who were more than two standard deviations below the mean on standardized intelligence tests (12). It has also been shown that there is no catch-up growth or improved performance in the neonatal period (9). Serious dysmorphogenesis of the neuronal and glial elements starts before 80 days of gestation, as shown by the absence of the corpus callosum (16). Furthermore, postnatal weight gain is poor, and the tremulousness and hyperactivity persist.

Considering cranial facial anomalies, short palpebral fissures are one of the common features. (Fig. 2). This occurred in 35 of 38 cases in Hanson's series (9). Because these infants have microphthalmia, it has been postulated that this may be a cause of the short palpebral fissures. Additionally, there is a midfacial hypoplasia in 28 of 40

FIGURE 2

Common Abnormalities in Fetal Alcohol Syndrome*	
Abnormality	No. Affected/No. Observed (%)
Growth and performance	
Prenatal growth deficiency‡	38/39(97)
Postnatal growth deficiency‡	37/38(97)
Microcephaly‡	38/41(93)
Developmental delay or mental deficiency‡	31/35(89)
Fine motor dysfunction	28/35(80)
Craniofacial	
Short palpebral fissures‡	35/38(92)
Midfacial hypoplasia	26/40(65)
Epicanthic folds	20/41(49)
Limb	
Abnormal palmar creases	20/41(49)
Joint anomalies (mostly minor)	17/41(41)
Other	
Cardiac defect (mostly septal defects)	20/41(49)
External genital anomalies (minor)	13/41(32)
Hemangiomas (mostly small, raised, strawberry angiomas)	12/41(29)
Ear anomalies (minor)	9/41(22)

*Data taken from 41 patients, including 11 whose cases were previously reported. [1,2]
‡ 2 SDs or more below the normal for age; equivalent to below the 2.5 percentile.
‡ Judging from standards of Chouke. [12]

Reprinted with permission of the JAMA, 235:1458, April 1976.

cases, or 65%, and epicanthal folds in 20 of 41 patients, or 49%. In Fig.3, taken from Rosett, the following characteristic facial dysmorphologic features are demonstrated (1). This infant has small palpebral fissures, microcephaly, flattened maxillary areas, a poorly developed filtrum, and a thin upper lip.

Limb deformities are another characteristic feature associated with fetal alcohol syndrome (Fig.2). These children showed abnormal palmar creases in 20 of 41 infants, or 49%, and joint anomalies were manifested in 17 of 41, or 41%. Perhaps the joint anomalies may be due to improper development of the central nervous system or due to some other neurologic impairment.

Regarding other anomalies (Fig. 2), cardiac anomalies must be considered, and this occurred in 20 of 41, or 49% of Hanson's series. Because most of these are septal defects, they should be considered major abnormalities. Abnormalities of the external genitalia were present in 13 of 41, or 32%, hemangiomas in 12 of 41 infants, or 29%, and ear anomalies in 9 of 41, or 22%.

FIGURE 3

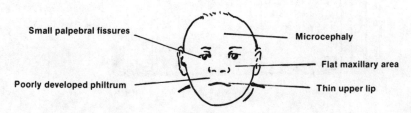

Characteristic facial dysmorphology of patients with fetal alcohol snydrome.

Frequency of anomalies is clearly influenced by the amount of drinking. Recall that in Ouellette's study (3), group one patients were abstainers or drank less than once a month, and group three drinkers averaged 45 ml of absolute alcohol per day. The group two category fell between group three and group one. Comparing the abstainers, group one, with group three, there are some remarkable differences (Fig. 4). For example, in group three, approximately 18% had major anomalies, compared to about 4% in group one. Also, in group three, 14% had minor anomalies, compared to about 5% in group one.

FIGURE 4

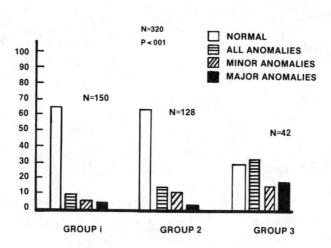

Frequency of Congenital Anomalies in Newborn infants.
Infants of heavy drinkers had more congenital anomalies, single and multiple, minor and major.

Reprinted with permission of the NEW ENGLAND JOURNAL OF MEDICINE, 297:528-530, September 1977.

Prevention of Fetal Alcohol Effects

Prevention of fetal alcohol effects involves three spheres: education, identification of problem patients, and counseling of problem patients. These patients should be counseled to cut down even in the third trimester of pregnancy. Identification of problem drinkers is difficult because many of them exercise the mechanism denial and are not willing to admit that they have a problem with alcohol. Rosett et al. (1) designed a simple ten question history (Fig. 5). The questionnaire is straightforward and comes under three categories: beer, wine, and liquor. Under each category, the patient is asked how many times she drinks each week, how many drinks she has each time, and if she ever drinks more. The tenth question "Has your drinking changed in the past year?" is of critical significance.

Russell and Bigler used a 31-item self-administered test (2). They also did blood alcohol levels on 12% of their patients, but it was found that this was not useful. The physicians themselves also administered a six-item test. These researchers found that the physician's test was the least reliable because patients want the approval of their physicians and tend to bias their answers. They found that the self-administered test was the best for identifying problem drinkers.

FIGURE 5

Beer: How many times per week _____
           How many cans each time _____
           Ever drink more? _____

Wine: *How many times per week* _____
           How many glasses each time _____
           Ever drink more? _____

Liquor: *How many times per week* _____
           How many drinks each time _____
           Ever drink more? _____

Has your drinking changed during the past year?

Ten-question drinking history (TQDH) for prenatal use.

Do Interventions Help?

Data clearly show that interventions do help and that if patients will cut down their drinking even in the third trimester, the outlook for the fetus can be improved considerably. Rosett et al. compared abstainers or reduced drinkers to a group of continued heavy drinkers (Fig. 6) (4). Though the populations were small, 15 and 27, the results were revealing. In the abstainers, 7% of the infants had major anomalies, compared to 15% in the continued heavy drinkers. One can see that the percentile for small-for-gestational-age was high in the continued drinkers, 37%; the premature rate was high, 26%; weight below the tenth percentile was calculated at 11%; and the head circumference at less than the tenth percentile was 33%. Jitteriness in the newborn period was 13% in the abstainers, compared to 41% in the continued heavy drinkers.

FIGURE 6

Relationship between clinical status of offspring of heavy drinkers and change in alcohol consumption before 3rd trimester.

	Abstained or Reduced Drinking, N-15	Continued Heavy Drinking, N-27
Major Congenital Anomalies	7%	15%
SGA (small for gestational age)		37%
Premature		26%
Wt. Less Than 10th Percentile		41%
Head Circumference Less Than 10th Percentile	33%	
Jittery	13%	41%

In another study, Rosett (Fig. 7) compared mothers who continued drinking heavily to those who reduced their drinking before the end of the third trimester (1). He found that the birth weights were below the tenth percentile in 45% of the infants of the continued drinkers, compared to 8% of the mothers who lessened their drinking before the third trimester. The length of the infant was below the tenth percentile in 20% of the continued heavy drinkers, compared with 4% in those who reduced drinking before the third trimester. Head circumference was below the tenth percentile in 27% of the infants of the heavy drinkers, compared to 4% of those who reduced drinking before the end of the third trimester.

FIGURE 7

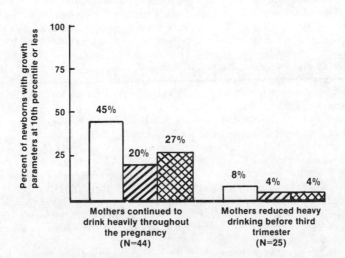

Reduction of heavy drinking with benefits to the newborn. Growth parameters: offspring born to women who reported heavy drinking at registration (N = 69). Open bar = weight at tenth percentil or less; slashed bar = length at tenth percentile or less; crossed bar = head circumference at tenth percentil or less.

Reprinted with permission of the American College of Obstetricians and Gynecologists (OBSTET. GYNECOL. 57:1-7, January 1981).

These data clearly demonstrate that the incidence of low birth weight and microcephaly can be reduced by reduction of alcohol consumption during pregnancy. In our society, where alcohol seems to be a way of life, it behooves all of us health professionals to identify the problem drinker, to educate, and to counsel our patients to reduce alcohol intake during pregnancy. As you all know, in the evolutionary process, the human brain has been growing for centuries. Though alcohol may be delightful to consume, we must advise reducing its use, lest we produce a generation of microcephalics, thus reversing the trend of normal evolution.

References

1. Rosett, H.L., Weiner, L., Edelin, K.C. Strategies for prevention of fetal alcohol effects. *Obstetrics and Gynecology*, 1981, 57, 1-7.
2. Russell, M., Bigler, L. Screening for alcohol-related problems in an outpatient obstetric-gynecologic clinic. *American Journal of Obstetrics and Gynecology*, 1979, 134, 4-12.
3. Ouellette, E.M., Rosett, H.L., Rosman, P., Weiner, L. Adverse effects of offspring of maternal alcohol abuse during pregnancy. *New England Journal of Medicine*, 1977, 297, 527-530.
4. Rosett, H.L., Ouellette, E.M., Weiner, L., Owens, E. Therapy of heavy drinking during pregnancy. *Obstetrics and Gynecology*, 1978, 51, 41-46.
5. Waltman, R. Iniquez. Placental transfer of ethanol and its elimination at term. *Obstetrics and Gynecology*, 1972, 40, 180-185.
6. Favre-Tissot, M., Delatour, P. Psychopharmacologie et teratogenese a propos du disulfiram: Essol experimental. *Annals Medico-Psychologiques*, 1965, 1, 635-740.
7. Nora, A.H., Nova, J.I., Blu, J. Limb reduction anomalies in infants born to disulfiram-treated alcoholic mothers. *Lancet*, 1977, 2, 664.
8. Hanson, J.W., Streissguth, A.P., Smith, D.W. The effects of moderate alcohol consumption during pregnancy on fetal growth. *Journal of Pediatrics*, 1978, 92, 457-460.
9. Hanson, J.W., Jones, K.L., Smith, D.W. Fetal alcohol syndrome: Experience with 41 patients. *Journal of the American Medical Association*, 1976, 235, 1458-1460.
10. Brandt, I. Brain growth, fetal malnutrition, and clinical consequences. *Journal of Prenatal Medicine*, 1981, 1,3.
11. Jones, K.L., Smith, D.W. Recognition of the fetal alcohol syndrome in early infancy. *Lancet*, 1973, 2, 999-1001.
12. Clarren, S.K., Smith, D.W. Fetal alcohol syndrome. *New England Journal of Medicine*, 1978, 298, 1063-1067.

Chapter Four
Familial Patterns of Alcoholism

Migs Woodside

Alcoholism causes family problems and, particularly, problems for children. Certain difficulties are environmental and may result from the tensions, inconsistencies, and pain experienced by living with an alcoholic parent. Usually, children of alcoholics do not know that alcoholism is a disease and may feel guilty and responsible for their parent's drinking. Youngsters also commonly feel invisible, neglected, and unloved because all family life revolves around the alcoholic. Often, children become confused and fearful when observing bizarre parental behavior during hallucinations or the memory lapses caused by alcoholic blackouts. Because parental alcoholism is a secret both within the family and outside of it, youngsters are made partners in the family's denial that a parent is drinking. They are afraid to reveal the problems that parental alcohol abuse causes them due to the stigma society attaches to alcoholism. Although the effects of family life on youngsters appear to have a major effect on their own high risks of future alcoholism, it is also true that inherited factors may be equally important.

At this time, however, the questions are myriad but the answers are few, and there is comparatively little research about children of alcoholics. A primary reason for the dearth of knowledge is that, until recently, research in this area lagged far behind research efforts on other alcohol problems. In eighteenth century England, concern was generated about parental drinking due to a rise in infant mortality and a decrease in the birth rate. Later, in the nineteenth century, the disease concept of alcoholism was developed and there was increased awareness of familial alcoholism and its possible damage to children.

However, earlier in this century, with the rise of psychoanalytic thought and emphasis on learned behavior, there was a dramatic shift of interest to the importance of role models, imitation of parental behavior, and environmental influences. At present, there is renewed interest in studies of genetic and biomedical factors. A few investigations are being performed on young children of alcoholics who have never consumed alcoholic beverages (1,2). A significant finding of the studies is that these youngsters, when given the same tests as adult alcoholics, show similar physiological responses to those of alcoholic adults.

An important milestone in research on children of alcoholics was the 1980 report by the Institute of Medicine,"Alcoholism, Alcohol Abuse and Related Problems: Opportunities for Research,"which identified this high-risk group as a population warranting further study (3). As a follow-up to the IOM report, the 1983 Research Planning Panel of the National Institute of Alcohol Abuse and Alcoholism likewise recommended familial transmission of alcoholism as an important area for further investigation (4).

Another significant event in research on children of alcoholics took place in April, 1984, when the Children of Alcoholics Foundation brought together 18 of the nation's leading scientists and clinical authorities to develop an agenda of research needs and fruitful opportunities for future study. Two publications have resulted from the meeting and conference findings encouraged funding authorities, research institutes, foundations, universities, and scientists to focus greater attention on children of alcoholics.

However, though this recent activity is encouraging, it is still meager in relationship to the many unanswered questions that exist. Some of the major questions to be answered include:

1. How is alcoholism transmitted? Is alcoholism learned through environment or is it controlled by heredity? Is alcoholism a combination of both? If alcoholism is transmitted by both heredity and environment, which factors are the most dominant and why?

2. What is actually transmitted from one generation to the next? Though it is unlikely that there is specific DNA or a gene for alcoholism as exists for blue eyes or red hair, one can inherit a predisposition to alcoholism or a readiness to inherit the disease. What principles or substances are at work in this transmission and

predisposition?

3. Can alcoholism be predicted? Can a predisposition to the disease be identified in advance? If so, what factors must be present and what techniques are needed for identification?

4. If alcoholism can be predicted, can it also be prevented? What is the most crucial period for intervention? What methods are the most effective in prevention?

It is a widely held belief that alcoholism runs in families and, indeed, research confirms this view. In fact, studies reveal that sons of alcoholic fathers are four times more likely than other sons to become future alcoholics (5, 6, 7); daughters of alcoholic mothers are three times more likely to become alcoholics than other women (8); grandsons of alcoholic grandfathers are at three times the risk of future alcoholism than others (9); and, daughters of alcoholics tend to marry alcoholic men (10), thereby the cycle is perpetuated in future generations. Because research also indicates that not all children of alcoholics will become future alcoholics, another fruitful issue for future exploration must be raised. What happens to those youngsters in an alcoholic family who do not become alcoholic? What protective barriers are at work that keep them from developing alcoholism? What alternative problems or lack of difficulties exist for them as adults?

Various methods have been used in research attempts to untangle the intermixture of heredity and environment. Methodology includes studies of twins, adoptees, and half siblings.

Twin Studies

The twin method enables scientists to compare identical or monozygotic (MZ) twins (having 100% of their gene pool in common) to fraternal or dizygotic (DZ) twins (who share only an average of 50% of their gene pool). This model permits a comparison of inheritance patterns and similarities (concordance rates) for various characteristics between the two twin types.

Kaij (11), in a study of 174 Swedish male twins where at least one twin in each pair was alcoholic, found that identical twins were more similar for alcoholism (59% concordance rate) than fraternal twins (28% concordance rate) and concluded that when one identical twin was alcoholic, the other identical twin was also more likely to be alcoholic than was the case in fraternal twin pairs. It should also be noted that the higher concordance rate in identical twins was particularly evident in cases of severe, chronic alcoholism.

A study by Hrubec and Omenn examined the medical records of male twins in the armed forces where at least one twin in each pair was diagnosed as alcoholic (12). Findings confirmed that the 241 pairs of identical twins were more similar for alcoholism (26.3 % concordance rate) than the 444 pairs of fraternal twins (11.9% concordance rate) and that identical twin pairs were more prone to alcoholic psychosis and liver cirrhosis than fraternal twins, pointing to organ-specific complications of alcoholism as well as to its genetic predisposition.

Twin studies, then, seem to confirm the inherited basis of alcoholism, yet several caveats exist. First, neither of these examples (nor other twin studies) use the same definitions of alcoholism or the same diagnostic criteria. Consequently, it is impossible to compare study results accurately. Second, twin studies do not account for any intrauterine variations, yet differences in prenatal environments may well be operational and important. Further, twin studies do not investigate factors at work after birth, although identical twins live together as adults more often than do fraternal twins. This leads to the possibility that identical twins may be more similar than fraternal twins in their drinking practices as a result of living together and having the opportunity to acquire each other's habits at an early age.

Adoption Studies

These studies are based on adoption records in Sweden and Denmark and are designed to investigate those children of alcoholic biological parents who were adopted and raised by other families. This model permits analysis of inherited and environmental influences when youngsters reach adulthood. Goodwin studied 55 sons of alcoholics who were removed from their biological families within 6 weeks after birth and adopted by nonalcoholic families. Goodwin compared them with 78 adopted sons who were not children of alcoholics (5,6,7,). The data indicate that the sons of alcoholic fathers were four times more likely than the other sons to become future alcoholics, although they were not reared in alcoholic adoptive homes. As adults, the sons of alcoholics developed alcoholism at an early age (by their late twenties) and their alcoholism was severe enough to require hospitalization. Goodwin also compared the sons who remained with their alcoholic biological parents and who were reared in an alcoholic family environment to their brothers who were adopted and raised by nonalcoholic families. Findings show that those sons who were reared by their alcoholic biological parents were no more likely to be alcoholic than were their brothers who were given up for adoption. These results point to an inherited predisposition to alcoholism, which is unaffected by the fact of living with an alcoholic parent.

Bohman, in a study of 913 Swedish women adopted by nonrelatives, found that daughters of alcoholic biological mothers were three times more likely than other women to become alcoholics and that their alcoholism was of a moderate, mild type (8). Cloninger investigated both sons and daughters of alcoholics who had been adopted and found that, as adults, their risk of alcoholism increased only when their original biological parent was alcoholic, regardless of any alcoholism among their adoptive parents (13). In this study, two distinct types of alcoholism were also identified: "milieu limited" and "male limited." When "milieu limited" alcoholism, the more mild, moderate form, is found in fathers, it is closely associated with mild alcohol abuse in sons or daughters. In contrast, "milieu limited" alcoholism in mothers is closely associated with mild alcohol abuse solely in daughters. "Male limited" alcoholism, which has a high correlation with criminality and severe alcoholism, appears to be transmitted by fathers to sons. Even when sons of "male limited" alcoholic fathers were adopted and reared by nonalcoholic families, they were still at nine times the risk of alcoholism than other sons where no alcoholism existed.

Adoption studies underline the importance of inherited factors transmitted by alcoholic biological parents to children, and seem to obviate environmental influences. Yet, findings in adoption studies are also inconclusive. In reviewing Goodwin's study of sons of alcoholic biological parents, there is little information presented about the family of origin, and whether one or two parents were the alcohol abusers. The criterion used to define parental alcoholism was the fact of hospitalization for that condition. It is possible that some alcohol-abusing parents were unidentified because they had never been hospitalized for the condition. Similarly, although data show that the adoptive families of the 55 sons of alcoholic biologic parents were not themselves hospitalized for alcoholism, there is no information as to whether or not they may have been abusing alcohol to some degree.

There are problems, too, in the studies of daughters of alcoholic biological mothers because the effects of maternal alcoholism on the fetus are unexplored. In addition, it is yet unknown if maternal alcoholism influences a child's future use of alcohol or causes a predisposition to alcoholism in adulthood. Another issue for examination is the finding that women appear more prone to a milder, moderate form of alcoholism than men. This raises additional questions about the possibility that severe alcoholism in men may be controlled by physiological and metabolic mechanisms. A further area for inquiry entails review of any protective cultural and social barriers that may keep women from becoming severe alcoholics.

Half-Sibling Studies

The purpose of the half-sibling method is similarly to separate genetic and environmental aspects of alcoholism. A study by Schuckit of 164 half-siblings, of whom 69 were alcoholic, showed as inconsequential the fact of being raised by an alcoholic parental figure, or step-parent (14). What was crucial, however, was whether or not a sibling had an alcoholic biological parent. Though 14% of the half-siblings who did not have alcoholic parents actually became alcoholic, this is a relatively small number in comparison with 50% of the children of alcoholic biological parents who became alcoholics, even when they were raised apart from that parent. The results of this half-sibling investigation weigh heavily in favor of inherited factors. However, the data (when more closely analyzed) show that in childhood, 81% of the alcoholic half-siblings lived in broken homes, raising the issue of the effects of divorce on future alcoholism. Further, the half-sibling study broadly defines alcoholism as drinking in a way that interferes with one's life, a very general criterion as compared with the adoption study's definition of alcoholism as hospitalization. It is evident that twin, adoption, and half-sibling reports do not employ common denominators for criteria, terminology, or populations, and this serves to invalidate accurate comparisons of study results and findings.

Recently, researchers have begun to adapt the family history method as a way to observe familial patterns of alcoholism. In performing family studies, investigators look at first-degree relatives, including parents, brothers, sisters, and children, and often extend their reviews to second-degree relatives: grandparents, aunts, and uncles. Some conclusions are that, in general, a higher rate of alcoholism exists in women's families (15), and that female alcoholics are twice as likely as male alcoholics to have been reared by two alcoholic parents (16). Other relatives are also key players—uncles in particular—and there is a close association between male alcoholics with alcoholic maternal uncles and a similar association between female alcoholics with alcoholic paternal uncles (17). Male alcoholics also have an association with alcoholism in their father's father (18), and it has been found that grandsons of alcoholic grandfathers were three times more likely to become alcoholics than other males by the time they were in their fifties(9).

In conclusion, though all of the studies described bring us closer to finding valuable answers about alcoholism issues, they also raise many critical questions for further exploration. Future research efforts may well be based on an interactive model that includes both inherited and environmental factors. It is possible that some types of alcoholism, such as "male limited", may be more genetically controlled. Still other types, such as "milieu limited," may be more related to environmental influences. As suggested by the 1983 Research Planning Panel of the National Institute of Alcohol Abuse and Alcoholism, alcoholism may arise from a biological vulnerability combined with a psychosocial risk (4). In using a comprehensive definition, future efforts may be directed towards finding new models and new techniques to investigate alcoholism. It is possible that by basing future research on a bio-behavioral/conceptual model, heredity and environment may finally be investigated together and we may begin to unlock the secrets of family alcoholism.

References

1. Begkiter, H., Porjesz, B., and Kissin, B. Brain dysfunction in alcoholics with and without family history of alcoholism. *Alcoholism: Clinical and Experimental Research*, 1982, 6(1), 136.

2. Gabrielli, W., Mednick, S., Volavka, J., Pollolk, V., Schulsinger, F., and Itil, T. Electro-encephalagrams in children of alcoholic fathers, *Psychophysiology*, 1982, 19(4), 404-407. 1982, 19(4), 404-407.

3. Institute of Medicine. *Alcoholism, Alcohol Abuse and Related Problems: Opportunities for Research.* Division of Health Promotion and Disease Prevention, National Academy Press, Washington, D.C., 1980.

4. National Institute on Alcohol Abuse and Alcoholism. Report of the 1983 research planning panel. Alcohol, Drug Abuse and Mental Health Administration, U.S. Department of Health and Human Services.

5. Goodwin, D., Schulsinger, F., Hermansen, L., Guze, S., and Winokur, G. Alcohol problems in adoptees raised apart from biological parents. *Archives of General Psychiatry*, 1973, 28, 238-243.

6. Goodwin, D. Adoption studies of alcoholism. *Journal of Operational Psychiatry*, 1976, 7.

7. Goodwin, D. *Is Alcoholism Hereditary?* Oxford University Press, New York, 1976.

8. Bohman, M., Sigvardsson, S., and Cloninger, R. Maternal inheritance of alcohol abuse. *Archives of General Psychiatry*, 1981, 38(9), 965-969.

9. Kaij, L. and Dock, J. Grandsons of alcoholics. *Archives of General Psychiatry*, 1975, 32, 1379-1381.

10. Nici, J. Wives of alcoholics as "repeaters." *Journal of Studies on Alcohol.*, 1979, 40, 677-682.

11. Kaij, L. Alcoholism in twins studies on the etiology and sequels of abuse of alcohol. Department of Psychiatry, University of Lund, Sweden, 1960.

12. Hrubec, Z., and Omenn G. Evidence of genetic predisposition to alcoholic cirrhosis and psychosis. *Alcoholism: Clinical and Experimental Research*, 1981, 5, 50, 207-215.

13. Cloninger, R. Genetic and environmental factors in the development of alcoholism. *Journal of Psychiatric Treatment and Evaluation*, 1983, 5.

14. Schuckit, M., Goodwin, D., and Winokur, G. A Study of alcoholism in half-siblings. *American Journal of Psychiatry*, 1972, 128.

15. Cotton N. The familial incidence of alcoholism. A review. *Journal of Studies on Alcohol*, 1979, 40, 89-116.

16. McKenna, T. and Pickens, R. Alcoholic children of alcoholics. *Journal of Studies on Alcohol*, 1981, 42, 1021-1029.

17. Stabenau, J. and Hesselbrock, V. Family pedigree of alcoholic and control patients. *International Journal of the Addictions*, 1983, 18.

18. Schuckit, M. A study of young men with alcoholic close relatives. *American Journal of Psychiatry*, 1982, 139.

Chapter Five
Children in Alcoholic Families

Michael Liepman, M.D., William Taylor White, M.S.N., and Ted D. Nirenberg, Ph.D.

Introduction

In the United States, there are an estimated 6.6 million children and another 22 million adults that have grown up in alcoholic homes (1,2). Recent Gallup polls have found as many as 33% of respondents reported their families were affected by alcohol problems (3,4). COAs comprise approximately 60% of all patients in chemical dependency programs, and they also show up as collaterals of others being treated for addictive disorders. COAs also appear in excess frequency among criminal justice offenders, mental health clientele, and hospital patients.

Alcohol, as a psychoactive drug, causes individuals to think, feel and behave differently in relation to the degree of intoxication. When a parent drinks heavily frequently, children learn to expect dramatic shifts in parental behavior. Eventually the child of an alcoholic parent (COA) learns to predict parental behavior or mood in relation to drinking status. To the child, the parent represents two very different people: a drinking parent and a sober parent, frequently as different as Jekyll and Hyde (5,6,7). If there is a chemically free parent in the home, this adult may also show shifts in mood and behavior corresponding to the drinking status of the other parent (8). Thus, the hallmark feature of parental behavior in alcoholic families is "consistent inconsistency" (9). Over the course of a single evening an alcoholic parent may alternatively be violent, overindulgent, and totally indifferent towards the children. Consequently, COAs seem to have difficulty understanding and accepting parental messages (10,11,12).

There is substantial evidence suggesting that COAs are at high risk for physical, psychological and social problems (13-21). If the mother drinks during pregnancy, the child may suffer from Fetal Alcohol Syndrome or fetal alcohol effects, which damage the developing fetus morphologically and interfere with the potential for subsequent normal postnatal physical (22,23) and intellectual development (24). Physical abuse or neglect may also occur after birth if alcohol abuse is associated with impairment of parenting (25-33). The alcoholic family may also impact negatively on the development of a child and adversely affect the child's self-esteem, personality and social behavior.

However, alcoholism treatment services overwhelmingly neglect services for COAs (34). A survey of NIAAA-funded alcoholism treatment programs reported that less than ten percent provide any therapy for family members (35). In order to receive adequate treatment services, children of alcoholics need to be seen and to be better understood by service providers.

This chapter attempts to identify the biological, psychological and social issues which differentiate children of alcoholics from other children, focusing on the clinically relevant factors. Essential treatment goals for COAs will be outlined, including ways to recruit their participation in treatment.

Risk of Addiction

Children of alcoholics are at considerable risk for developing alcohol (36-39) or other drug dependence (40-44). Both environmental and hereditary contributions to this excess risk are important, but the exact nature of their relative contributions has not been fully established.

One set of studies has focused on the differences between identical and fraternal twins who share, respectively, 100% versus 50% of the exact same genetic instructions for body structures and functions. If raised together in a similar environment, substantially greater concordance for alcoholism among identical twin pairs (70% versus 35%) supports the hypothesis of biological inheritance of predisposing factors for the alcoholic phenotype. It can be seen that environment is also important in that approximately 30% of male identical twins of alcoholics in these studies were able to avoid becoming alcoholic.

A second type of study contrasts the relative contributions of biological family history to the environmental impact of alcoholism in adoptive parents by studying adoptees. Goodwin and colleagues (45-47) studied two groups of Danish adoptees which were matched by age and circumstances of adoption but differed by alcoholism in biological parents. They found alcoholism in 18% of sons adopted from alcoholic parents versus 5% in sons adopted from nonalcoholic parents. For daughters, the differences were not significant. Despite evidence of more family problems and alcoholic role models in the home of the biological family of family history positive adoptees, nonadopted siblings of like gender had similar prevalence of alcoholism. Overall, the risk of alcoholism for both sons and daughters of alcoholic biological parents was roughly four times that found in the general population. In addition, the severity of the natural parents' alcoholism was correlated with severity of son's alcoholism, regardless of duration of exposure to the alcoholic parent. Sons of both alcoholic and nonalcoholic parents did not differ in drinking quantity and frequency. However, the drinking patterns of the adoptive parents influenced the drinking patterns of the adoptees. Hence, style of drinking is probably environmentally determined.

A similar study of Swedish adoptees found two distinct types of transmission of alcoholism (36-48). The most common type (75% of male alcoholics) was "milieu-limited" in which typically both parents had mild alcoholism without criminality, low social status of adoptive fathers, older age at placement, longer stay with biological mother, and longer postnatal hospitalization. In the remaining 25% of male alcoholics, they found "male-limited" inheritance in which typically the biological father, but not the mother, had alcoholism and criminality. The sons usually began to abuse alcohol in adolescence. Daughters in this study tended to inherit alcoholism by the milieu-limited pattern. Their risk of alcoholism was most substantial (four-fold) if their biological mothers had alcoholism.

Biological Differences of the COA

Several biological factors which have been associated with a family history of alcoholism will be discussed to show how they might predispose a person to develop alcoholism. These include, for example, (1) slow metabolism of acetaldehyde, (2) differences in brain electrophysiology, and (3) different subjective sensitivity to the intoxicating effects of alcohol.

Removal of acetaldehyde from the body after it is produced from breakdown of ethyl alcohol requires enzymatic conversion by aldehyde dehydrogenase. Rapid removal is thought to be protective, since acetaldehyde is quite toxic. While alcoholics are known to have slow removal of acetaldehyde (49-51), recent evidence suggests that sons of alcoholics (who are not yet alcohol abusers) may also eliminate acetaldehyde more slowly than sons without a family history of alcoholism (52). This finding suggests a genetic metabolic difference which may increase the risk of some drinkers to biological harm from excessive drinking. It may also explain why certain consequences of alcohol abuse are under genetic control. Chemical reaction of acetaldehyde with brain neurotransmitters has been hypothesized as an explanation of these risk differences (53,54).

Mounting evidence in animal experiments supports the theory that an opiate-like chemical produced in the brain as a result of the presence of acetaldehyde, called tetrahydropapaveroline (THP), induces uncontrolled ethanol self-administration (55,56). The theory predicts a vicious cycle in which drinkers who fail to rapidly detoxify excess acetaldehyde would suffer body damage and produce brain THP each time they drank. The latter would drive them to continue drinking despite the consequences. As long as such persons abstain from drinking, they prevent themselves from acetaldehyde-induced body damage and THP-induced urges to drink, but upon resumption of any drinking, the acetaldehyde would once again drive production of THP and the cycle would begin anew. If this theory is correct, persons without the hereditary defect in the enzyme aldehyde dehydrogenase would be able to drink without body damage and loss of control, hence without alcoholism.

The following electrophysiological differences in the brains of nonalcoholic sons of alcoholic fathers have also been noted:

1. Paucity of alpha-waves (which are usually considered signs of tranquility or relaxation) which can be restored to normal by small doses of alcohol (57-60); and

2. Differences in evoked brain potentials (brain waves associated with thoughts or sensations) which may indicate differences in brain structure or function (61). Translated into behavioral terms, these differences may produce anxiety, hyperactivity, poor impulse control, or intolerance of stress, all of which are features of COAs. The normalization of the alpha by low doses of alcohol is reminiscent of statements by many of our patients who say that drinking makes them feel normal; it calms or relaxes them. It is possible that these differences reflect genetic factors which cause increased risk of alcoholism, or they may reflect environmentally induced brain changes caused by living in an alcoholic home.

Two other factors associated with alcoholism and being a COA are MAO activity and zinc levels. Low platelet monoamine oxidase (MAO) activity in alcoholic probands is associated with a high proportion of alcoholic relatives, while high platelet MAO activity is associated with few alcoholic relatives (62,63). This suggests that an inherited form of alcoholism may be linked genetically with MAO activity. Depressed zinc levels have been found in 8-13 year old COAs of both genders prior to any use of alcohol (64). Depressed zinc levels have also been observed in drinking alcoholics, but the significance of this is unknown.

Inheritance of Psychiatric Disorders
Whether the association of alcoholism with hyperactivity (65-68) is hereditary or environmental remains controversial. However, there is little doubt that familial risk of these problems is higher among alcoholic families than in the general population. Many alcoholic patients refer to intrapsychic or social problems when explaining their drinking relapses. While these may not actually be causes of the drinking, they may increase the risk of relapse by making sober living unpleasant.

Developmental Stage-Specific Impacts
Growing up in an alcoholic home may impair the normal developmental process by exposing the child to extreme and/or inconsistent parental responses (71,74,75). The following section documents what is known and believed about the developmental impact of alcoholism in the family on children of all ages.

It has been proposed that the extent of developmental harm is inversely proportional to the child's age at onset of parental alcoholism. Fox (76) suggests that family alcoholism could interfere with mother-infant bonding, leading to permanent emotional scars which would influence the outcome of the remainder of development. Furthermore, Richards (77), contends that global denial of alcoholism and its behavioral consequences supported by both parents predisposes younger children to develop a faulty sense of reality, facilitating confusion, distrust, powerlessness and fear which could interfere with subsequent emotional growth. Chafetz (13) states that youngsters whose parents develop alcoholism during their child's adolescence have probably experienced healthier parenting and role-models than those whose parents abused alcohol when their child was younger. All adolescents have sober extra-parental adult role-models available if they look for them, but preschoolers are captives in the home. Children exposed to parental alcoholism at an earlier age also are more likely to be exposed to parental alcoholism longer than those whose parents began to abuse alcohol later. Nevertheless, careful scientific support of this belief has not been published.

Those who believe that most of the bad outcomes are genetically determined would not expect a differential outcome based on intensity or timing of social environmental factors. Some investigators believe, however, that there is a differential impact by the gender of the alcoholic parent and the ages of the child during the interval(s) of problematic drinking (78). Peitler (79) contrasted the psychological adjustment of two groups of adolescent sons of alcoholic fathers, one group experiencing the onset of paternal alcoholism before the age of seven. The sons in the onset-before-seven group were significantly more impaired than their counterparts on measures of self-esteem, social withdrawal and antisocial behavior.

Psychological growth of COAs may be impaired because of harmful environmental factors which lead to poor self-esteem (80), depression (81), anxiety disorders (20), emotional detachment, dependency, social aggression, emotional irritability, preoccupation with inner thoughts and anxiety (19), external locus of control (64,82), psychosomatic illness (21), impaired reality testing (77), guilt excesses (15), poor coping skills (83), denial of feelings, mistrust of others and abusive relationships (10). Bedwetting is quite common in male COAs (84).

Environmental influences on COAs include exposure to family instability (85), parental conflict or violence (15,26,86-90), social isolation or deviance (34,91,92), parental inconsistency (93,94), poor role models (13,95), and severe family stress (86). Social deviance may be reflected by aggression and delinquency (19,79,95) and poor school performance (14,96). Hyperactivity (97,98), especially in association with conduct disorders (99), may be environmentally and/or genetically influenced. In some COAs there is evidence of a post-traumatic stress disorder, usually triggered by one dramatic or chronic serial traumatic experience(s).

According to Erickson (100), healthy child development requires that youngsters master age-specific psychosocial crises. In this stepwise schema, infants must achieve a basic sense of trust, toddlers a sense of autonomy, preschoolers a sense of initiative, school age children a sense of industry, and adolescents reaffirm their autonomy. Adults also go through developmental stages, and usually use their parents (or their memory of their parents) as role models and supports for these stages. The following section outlines the impact that the alcoholic home environment may have on the major developmental tasks of children and adults through the lifespan.

Infants achieve trust through experiencing consistently satisfying nurturing relations with the mother figure. Sensitive parenting, available on demand, with a consistent style is essential to normal psychological development. Children who are severely neglected fail to eat and die; children who are moderately neglected may mistrust adults to meet their needs; and children who are inconsistently handled have difficulty establishing strong bonds to individuals (101). If the mother or father intermittently abuse alcohol frequently during infancy, they may respond to the infant's cries inconsistently due to marked differences in parental mood or level of consciousness associated with different degrees of intoxication. During intoxication, there may be insensitivity to the needs of the infant, and during withdrawal there may be irritability and intolerance. The inconsistent parenting characteristics of the alcoholic home may engender insecurity and mistrust in the newborn. Mood shifts and competing responsibilites in the sober spouse of an alcoholic and in the infant's siblings may also have some damaging effects on the developing infant.

Toddlers (1.5 to 3 years) must attain a sense of autonomy within the context of the security of parental controls. While fully aware that they are separate people, toddlers do not possess the cognitive capacity to rationalize life events. Toddlers experiment with doing things by themselves "their way". Alcoholic parental controls of toddlers may go to either extreme or may vacillate between both extremes. During withdrawal (hangovers) in some families and during intoxication (with poor control of temper) in others, the reaction to toddler developmental exploration may be excessively restrictive. Violent responses may terrify the toddler. Overprotectiveness by either parent may suppress experimentation which in turn may prevent experiencing the self-confidence that accompanies mastery of autonomous endeavors. Parental intoxication to stupor or prolonged absence from the home may leave the toddler unsupervised and at risk of physical and emotional harm. Unsupervised toddlers may undertake projects beyond their physical and intellectual capacities and thus may get into various types of trouble. They may end up feeling a lack of self-control. Confused toddlers come to feel inadequate and shameful for undertaking a normal developmental task. They are at risk of developing an operating belief that life is arbitrarily controlled by external forces and, consequently, exercise little self-control (64-80).

Preschoolers need to develop the initiative necessary to satisfy natural curiosity. They learn to distinguish reality from fantasy and try to understand the connections between events or causality. They challenge the patience of adults with playful limit testing and unending persistence. These youngsters require predictable, understanding parenting that rewards honesty, responsibility and goal-directed behavior. In alcoholic homes, the preschooler's constant "quest for answers" is often interpreted as intrusive or bothersome. During parental inebriation, questions may go unanswered or are handled abruptly. Limit testing by the child may be used by the parent to justify drinking binges and verbal or physical violence towards the child or others; or it may go unnoticed without any parental response.

A child's questions about drinking associated behaviors or events may trigger in the alcoholic parent 1) guilt-induced defensiveness in the form of projection of blame onto the child 2) denial of the event (it may be forgotten due to psychological repression or alcoholic mnesic "blackouts"), or 3) guilt-induced overcompensation in the form of lenience ("spoiling" the child). Depending upon the availability and quality of social support of family members and significant others, the child may learn from this experience 1) to mistrust the alcoholic parent and to lie about reality or 2) to mistrust his or her own perception of reality and remain living in a fantasy world. Such children become guilt-ridden and may begin to show signs of depression and low self-esteem (10,11). The child at this age usually identifies with parent figures in terms of values and behaviors, including attitudes towards alcohol and drinking associated behavior by both parents (102,103).

Preadolescent children (5-11 years) face the developmental challenge of industry versus inferiority. Enthusiastic about applying rapidly developing cognitive skills, these children aspire to demonstrate to adults their newly mastered learning in order to feel a sense of self-worth. Parental award for goal-directed behavior is critical. Significant parental involvement during this age is important for ongoing role modeling. Through identification with parental adults, these children continue to adopt social values and behavior.

In many alcoholic families the parental response to the enthusiasm of preadolescents is poor because the child's activities conflict with the family's pathological accommodation to the alcoholism. The alcoholic parent who is physicall gone or mentally incapacitated much of the time may be neither available to support the child in preparation for school, religious or sports activities nor to celebrate successful achievements. The lack of parental investment during this time may produce feelings of inferiority in the child, which may be heightened by parental projection or blaming. Frequent parental absence promotes the assumption of parenting roles by others (e.g., the other parent, grandparents, older siblings, other relatives or neighbors) who may teach the child different values than those espoused by the absent parent; parent-child conflict may arise when the alcoholic parent discovers that the child has invested heavily in different values. Identification with parental behavior, especially that observed when the parent is intoxicated, may produce anger in both parents as it affronts their wish to deny or rid the family of the alcoholism.

In families with an irritable alcoholic (some are irritable when withdrawing, others have a short fuse when intoxicated), attempts by family members to lessen family tension may force the preadolescent child to restrict home activities to quiet, isolating endeavors. This usually means no friends may visit. When an alcoholic parent unpredictably appears in an angry mood or with embarrassing, poorly controlled behavior, most families wish to conceal the problem from the community. They may isolate themsevles from others to avoid social stigma (75,104).

Poor self-concept and poor social skills coupled with the family deviance from community norms (which may also produce social stigma) may jeopardize peer relationships. Further, some children may sense that the alcoholic parent's behavior presents physical danger (of fire, violence, falls, child neglect of a younger sibling) and may result in school avoidance or inattention because of these worries. Hence, academic and social problems are common among COAs. Children who overconform to the strictest of parental rules may become similar to Wegscheider's (11) "lost child," while those who rebel to elicit attention may end up the family or community "scapegoat". The adolescent repeats the process of affirming autonomy and independence while moving through three stages: The first stage, usually at ages 12-14, is one of timid cooperation with parents and agreeing to their values; the second stage, usually at ages 14-17, is rebellion, where the teen rigidly rejects parental values and violates their rules to test self-determination and the dwindling influence of parental controls; and the last stage is maturity, normally ages 17-20, during which the young adult realizes that choices can be self-determined, whether or not they are in synchrony with parental values.

In the alcoholic family, teen misbehavior may be met with 1) no reaction due to parental insensitivity, absence or preoccupation, 2) overreaction due to guilt about past parenting inadequacy or fear of repetition of one's own problems in the next generation, or 3) inconsistent vacillation between these extremes. Ignoring teen violation of family rules often leads to more severe misbehavior in search of limits. If parental limits are not promptly set, the teen behaivor will eventually violate community standards and community authorities will become involved. On the other hand, overreaction to limit testing may precipitate counterviolence, running away from the family, or fearful cessation of natural social exploration. Some adolescents bury themselves in drugs as a way of blocking their perception of their family dilemma, and the result is maturational arrest. Many teens will identify with the alcoholic parent in selecting extra-parental adult figures and peers.

Adults continue to develop emotionally as they progressively leave home, become financially independent, start their own families, get jobs, raise and launch their children, become grandparents, retire, lose a spouse, sustain losses of body functions, and so forth (105). To some extent, adults respond in accordance with their recollection of how their own parents and other significant relatives of prior generations weathered the stresses of this process (106). Social support and advice in problem-solving may be sought from forebearers at times of crisis (107). Families usually influence the younger generation via family rituals (108); in the case of extended families that see each other quite often, the influence of elders may be extensive. Adults from alcoholic families attend family ritual celebrations and find themselves exposed to heavy drinking by at least one, if not more, ancestors and family friends. In this setting they might also begin or continue to drink heavily (109,110), or they might become concerned or embarrassed by the behavior of their family. Their role models may teach them to drink excessively in response to developmental stresses. Adult COAs also become embroiled in family controversies over how to deal with sick alcoholic relatives, whether to enable them to continue to drink or to encourage them to stop.

Recovering alcoholic COAs and their spouses find it particularly hard to deal with drinking alcoholic parents who may not support or understand their recovery attempts. Such parents may provoke urges in their recovering offspring by coaxing or daring them to take a drink, meanwhile belittling their drinking problem and recovery. In general, when recovery begins to take hold in part of an alcoholic family system, there is a tendency for it to spread to others just as the alcoholism spreads. Those who resist recovery often find themselves cut off from the recovery-committed relatives. In Wolin's terms, a "subsumptive" family must become a "distinctive" family if it is to maintain recovery despite others continuing to problem drink in the extended family system. Advice from elders on how to deal with grandchildren who are exposed to alcohol and other drugs may not be terribly helpful, especially if some of the middle generation turned out alcoholic. Typically in alcoholic family systems, the alcoholic parent disagrees with the non-alcoholic parent about the appropriateness of teen drinking, and the conflict is never resolved so that consistent parenting on that issue never occurs. In the subsequent generation, grandparents may take sides on the same issue and remain at an impasse.

Roles in Alcoholic Families

A role is an expected and repetitive set of behaviors enacted by an individual in a social context (111). Thornton and Nardi (112) stated that role expectations refer to (1) the ways in which a person should behave, (2) the particular attitudes and values appropriate to him/her, or (3) the knowledge and skills he/she should have. For young children, role expectations emanate from members of their immediate family who have a similar or a reciprocal role (113). For example, for a boy, other siblings would be in similar roles and parents would be in reciprocal roles in terms of parent-child issues, and males and females might split into similar and reciprocal roles over gender issues. The process of role acquisition in families is dynamic and interactive between the person acquiring the role and those who project their expectations.

Thornton and Nardi outline requirements for adults to develop healthy roles. First, the individual acquiring the role must be well-differentiated enough to influence the expectations of others.

Helpless youngsters must accept parental expectations no matter how unreasonable. In this way children may be programmed by parents who do not recognize their true strengths and weaknesses to pursue roles which may not be in their best interests. Some alcoholic families prescribe roles for the children which are a reaction to dissatisfaction with a parent (i.e., "You'll be a better cook than your mother") while others may force identification with a disliked family member (i.e., "You're just like your Uncle Charlie, the drunken bum!"). Ideally a child should be allowed to develop in a manner that compliments his temperament and inborn resources. Nardi (94) suggests that among COAs there is incongruence between personal traits and role performed which results in social and psychological maladjustment. In this regard, the locus of control of a child with an unnatural role might be externally based on the absence of self-determination, and such is frequently the case in COAs (64,82). People may not be mature enough until adulthood to divest themselves of imposed unnatural roles, and to do so usually requires some therapeutic assistance.

The second requirement of Thornton and Nardi is consistency of expectations. In any family, a child may encounter differences of expectations between various family members. In families with marital problems and in unstable or broken homes, where parental consensus has failed, the child may feel torn between conflicting expectations which, if persistent, may lead to personal ambivalence or low self-esteem. The child in an alcoholic family has to contend with another form of inconsistent expectations, those of parents who markedly alter their behavior from one extreme to the other, like Jekyll and Hyde, depending upon whether or not one parent has been drinking. In essence, the child is exposed to conflicting expectations coming from the same person at different times, possibly the very same day. Thus, in order to survive, the child learns to play different roles when the family alcoholic is drinking and when the alcoholic is sober. This shift in personal behaviors in direct response to parental drinking may influence a COA's perception that external forces largely control personal destiny.

Black (93), describes three typical COA role patterns: (1) the RESPONSIBLE ONE; (2) the ADJUSTER; and (3) the PLACATER. She contends that these roles confer survival benefit upon the child and family by compensating for family deficiencies and providing homeostatic balance. The RESPONSIBLE ONE provides structure and stability to a chaotic home, takes responsibility for the well-being of the entire family, including parents (role reversal). The child may take over parental instrumental tasks (e.g. cooking meals, caring for younger siblings, etc.) without overt parental assignment of these roles nor parental supervision. RESPONSIBLE ONES are prematurely thrust into a parental decision-making role where they must meet the needs of others and set aside personal emotional needs. They learn not to depend on others and to always be in control. They derive self-esteem from achievement, but often set themselves up for failure by taking on impossible tasks. As adults, they have difficulty achieving mutual intimacy in a marriage, and often become enablers for others with chemical dependencies. They may achieve leadership roles in their profession, but rarely achieve personal satisfaction from their jobs because of unrecognized unrealistic goals. They tend to blame themselves for their own shortcomings and events beyond their control. They are also prone to emotional depression. This role is most common in the eldest sibling.

The ADJUSTER finds safety in the alcoholic home by adjusting to whatever happens by suppressing thoughts and feelings and becoming resigned to an inevitable lack of control over the situation. Manipulated by parents and the RESPONSIBLE ONE, these children are followers who lack self-esteem and a sense of internal control. As adults, they remain followers, avoiding responsibility and leadership. They blame others for their lack of satisfaction with life.

The PLACATER smooths over conflicts in the tension-filled alcoholic home. Responding to guilt and anxiety over an irrational belief that he or she caused the parent's drinking problem, this child tries to calm distraught parents or divert their attention away from the crisis at hand. Black (10) quotes a five-year-old COA in the midst of a family disaster: "Don't worry Mom, I won't remember this when I grow up." As an adult, phobic of conflict, the PLACATER becomes a mediator, and usually fails to meet personal needs because of the strong desire to avoid anger. Also prone to depression, the PLACATER may suffer from passivity in relationships.

Wegscheider(11), describes four distinct COA roles which are quite similar to Black's three: (1) the CARETAKER (family hero); (2) the PROBLEM CHILD (family scapegoat); (3) the FORGOTTEN CHILD (lost child); and (4) the FAMILY PET (family mascot). These roles are also seen as necessary for survival in the alcoholic family during childhood. They continue into adulthood unless changed in therapy or when family structure changes, (i.e., children may switch roles or assume different roles when a child leaves home). Wegscheider's roles overlap with those of Black.

Family Dynamics

Historically, the family suffering from alcoholism in one of its members was considered to be passively victimized by the alcoholic's sins. But as the disease model took hold, various investigators examined the family from different perspectives. Sociologists who found differences when comparing families with an alcoholic

member to non-alcoholic families, and clinicians who saw pathological behavior in the wives of the alcoholics they were treating
engaged in scientific controversy over whether the wife's behavior
was causing the alcoholism or whether it was her way of adjusting to
the stresses of her husband's disease (114,115,116). Two common
roles for spouses are seen in alcoholic families. One involves the
spouse as a direct supporter of the drinking behavior, often as a
drinking partner. The other role has the spouse rejecting the
alcoholic and the drinking, while never effectively bringing the
alcoholism into remission. In the former role, COAs may learn that
the alcohol abuse is desirable since both parents seem to approve of
it. In the latter, the children may identify either with the rejecting or
the rejected parent. In either scenario, they may resent the enabling parent as much as the drinking parent.

Why would a family tolerate all this pain and suffering for
extended periods of time? Some suggested that denial of the
problem kept the family from taking action to rid itself of the
alcoholism. Others suggested that financial dependence held
wives of alcoholics to their sick husbands (117,118,119). Steinglass
(120,121), based upon direct observation of alcoholic couples during drinking and sobriety, concluded that the alcoholic's drinking
served a homeostatic or stabilizing function in the family. Shifts in
behavior associated with drinking and abstinence were present in
both members. This was confirmed by observations of whole
nuclear families (122-124). Specific roles within alcoholic families
may offer a means to withstand pain; though the roles may actually
serve to increase suffering in the long-term, the role-prescribed
behaviors may provide short-term comfort as a lesser of evils.

Stability of family roles over time despite extremely painful
consequences, and overt resistance to therapeutic attempts by
therapists and representatives of community agencies are consistent with Steinglass' conclusion. Without family therapy, most families would suffer serious "side-effects" if the alcoholic were to stop
drinking permanently. For example, if the alcoholic depends on
alcohol to relieve anxiety while expressing emotions, the family
encounters an anxious, emotionally withdrawn person whenever
he abstains from drinking. Until the next drinking episode, the
family receives no feedback, and the alcoholic accumulates unex-
pressed emotions which may be explosively released during the

next drunken episode. A form of Smilkstein's "pathological equilibrium" (107), this pattern demonstrates how the alcoholic's drinking serves a positive, stabilizing function for the family system, despite the "costs" to individual members of the system. This also explains why members of alcoholic families seem to act in ways which enable the drinking to continue, and may even provoke a relapse in the recovering alcoholic (125-128).

Minuchin (129), notes that while a healthy family is able to alter its response to stress flexibly, an alcoholic family can exercise only "wet" or "dry" behavior in a stressful situation until recovery. Then they only have "dry" behavior. Unless family therapy is used to increase family flexibility, the recovering alcoholic family would most likely suffer one of three outcomes: 1) relapse of the alcoholic, 2) family break-up, or 3) replacement of the alcoholic in the sick role by another family member (5). Since individual treatment of any member of an alcoholic family for any psychological problem related even indirectly to the family alcoholism may result in any of these three outcomes, the therapist should be wary of treating the "patient" in a vacuum without considering the potential family consequences of the therapy and without offering to treat or refer the family for family therapy, should the need and opportunity arise.

The roles of the COAs during childhood may be carried into adult family life by both genetic and behavioral routes to produce another alcoholic family. Assortative mating, selecting a mate from an alcoholic family, may increase the genetic risk of passing the predisposition on to the next generation. The reciprocal behaviors which complement the COA roles are consistent with alcohol or drug abuse. The creation of another alcoholic family in the next generation may also be generated by enabling behaviors in the ancestors and family rituals (109,110). When the alcoholic parent dies or recovers, rather than shed the familiar role, the COA may seek associations with other alcohol or drug abusers to replace the alcoholic parent.

Recruiting Family Involvement

Getting family members to participate in alcoholism treatment is not always easy (130). When the setting is an alcohol treatment program, there is a tendency for exasperated relatives to drop the intoxicated alcoholic at the door, hoping he or she will return home sober after treatment. They may not even visit. Likewise, when family problems arise in other settings, such as school problems in a COA, it is often difficult to get the alcoholic parent involved. By insisting that the family attend one session altogether as a family, one may increase the chances of involving the family in recovery. At times the therapist must refuse to offer treatment under any other conditions in order to motivate reluctant relatives to participate and the alcoholic to permit their involvement. In school or court settings, threats of alternative consequences (6) may be the only way to obtain family cooperation. This may be justifiable if one believes that interventions without family involvement are rarely successful.

Initiating Change

It is not easy to alter a family life-course which has persisted for decades or generations. Those in the family who suffer most from their role-determined behavior may be most interested in change, but unless the entire family cooperates in the change process, even those members are unlikely to change. A first step in modifying the family process is to assemble the entire family and to interest them in participating in recovery. By finding out how they suffer, and who suffers in which ways, one can begin to offer hope that the suffering can stop simply by trying the therapist's suggestions. It is also necessary to recruit their participation by making them feel that their contribution to the therapy is important and relevant (131). Age-appropriate ways to maximize their input and participation must be provided. Furthermore, they must be told that if certain members of the family refuse to participate in therapy, there is danger of undermining it. Those who decide to work towards recovery must be warned of this, so that they can take steps to reduce the influence of the resistent members of the family.

Before one begins to do therapy with alcoholic families, it is often helpful to expose them to basic education about their illness. This can be done by exposing them to classes, films, books or by teaching the family during family sessions. Learning about the typical alcoholic family rules and roles gives the therapist and family members a common vocabulary and conceptual basis to discuss their issues. It is amazing to see patients discover for the first time that their own private misery is shared by millions of others as they read a story similar to their own in books, watch someone like themselves on a movie screen, or hear their story delivered by a total stranger at an AA, Al-Anon, Alateen or therapy group. Goals of education for COAs include learning about the disease concept so they can stop feeling guilt over the alcoholic behavior of their parent(s), realizing which of their family rules and roles are healthy and unhealthy, and discovering that there are other ways to cope with problems than what they have observed in their families. They may also find a new level of love and concern from fellow patients that overcomes their mistrustful and isolating defensive style.

The COAs in the family, young and old, need to be identified so that their special needs can be addressed. Their reluctance to trust can interfere with the therapeutic relationship. Often they begin to trust other COAs before they trust anyone else, so involvement in role-specific groups (e.g. Alateen, Alatots, therapy or play groups for young COAs, Adult COA Al-Anon) can be a helpful adjunct to the therapy by providing a destigmatized forum in which COAs can begin to open themselves up to other people and to recovery. Once trust and credibility are established, COAs must be shown that while their current behavior derives from past attempts to survive in a sick environment, this behavior is no longer necessary, and may be harmful.

Open and honest expression of feelings is often difficult at first, and is facilitated by teaching them to recognize and name their different feelings, and to express them in a way that optimizes clarity and minimizes hurting others. Learning social interactive skills usually helps to channel negative feelings into effective constructive action. Most important of all is helping CoAs to realize their own importance. Breaking through the guilt and stigma and unmasking the people behind all the unhealthy behavior is a major task for any therapist, yet when this is accomplished, the results can be astonishing.

Verbal therapy techniques may be inadequate to meet the challenge of alcoholic families. Some members, including young children and those with cognitive deficits, lack high levels of verbal skills. Furthermore, expression of feelings though verbal means may be forbidden by unspoken family rules (104). By using gestalt projective techniques which encourage acting out problematic roles and behaviors in play or with toy puppets (132,133), the use of psychodrama (134), or family sculpting (75), art expressive therapy (135), response to the Family Relations Indicator (136), or to emotion evoking films, children and adults can overcome their inhibitions and express and communicate their feelings to one another as a sober family, often for the very first time. Feedback from therapist home or office observation, or even better, watching a videotaped visit of the family while the alcoholic is intoxicated can be used to overcome denial and facilitate more honest and realistic communication within the sober family about the other side of their Jekyll and Hyde life together. Once this begins, the family tends to get healthier, and generally refuses to return to blocked communication patterns. Multiple family groups focusing on alcoholism recovery with emphasis on feelings can also make it easier for shy members to speak out once they realize that they are not alone in their predicament.

It is important to introduce early some behavioral change assignments for the families so that they can overcome pessimism and invest their energy in striving towards long-term recovery. Small incremental family cooperation tasks such as ceasing blaming each other, altering role assignments, revealing secrets or regularly expressing positive feelings to one another may help to begin the recovery.

Individual treatment of COAs may be necessary at some point in their recovery from being alcoholism-affected. Many of the issues to be addressed in such treatment are discussed in another chapter of this book (Cable, Noel & Swanson). COA issues may interfere with the psychotherapeutic relationship if trust is a problem. Depression, poor self-esteem and passivity may block investment in therapy and change. Impulsivity or lack of persistence may lower attendance at therapy sessions. Belief in an external locus of control may block taking responsibility for personal behavior; belief in responsibility for the behavior of others may distract the CoA from focusing on changing his own behavior. Intoxication with alcohol or other mind-altering drugs will interfere with experiencing one's feelings and learning to cope with them.

Summary

Alcoholic families raise their children to accommodate to the unhealthy behaviors of the alcohol abuser and all who enable its persistence in the family. These children are at risk for both hereditary and learned behavioral problems which may continue through the generations. The children learn to survive in the sick family by acquiring behavioral roles at some cost to personal freedom and mental health. The children may find it difficult to shed these roles during the parent's alcoholism recovery. The most effective way to alter the course of these problems in COAs is treatment, especially with family involvement if possible.

References

1. Russell, M., Henderson, C., & Blume, S.B. *Children of Alcoholics: A Review of the Literature.* New York: Children of Alcoholics Foundation, 1985.
2. Woodside, M. *Children of Alcoholics.* New York: The New York State Division of Alcoholism and Alcohol Abuse, 1982.
3. Gallup Organization Inc. *American Families 1982.* Princeton, NJ: Gallup Organization Inc., 1982.
4. Gallup Organization Inc. *American Families 1984.* Princeton, NJ: Gallup Organization Inc., 1984.
5. Liepman, M.R., Nirenberg, T.D., & White, W.T. Family-oriented treatment of alcoholism, *Rhode Island Medical Journal,* 1985, 68(3), 123-126.
6. Liepman, M.R., Wolper, B., & Vazquez, J. An ecological approach for motivating women to accept treatment for drug dependency. In B.G. Reed, G.M. Beschner, & J. Mondonaro (Eds.) *Treatment Services for Drug Dependent Women (Vol. 2).* NIDA Treatment Research Monograph Series, DHHS Publication No. [ADM] 82-1219. Washington, DC: US Government Printing Office, 1982.
7. Royce, J.E. *Alcohol Problems and Alcoholism. A Comprehensive Survey.* New York: MacMillan Publishing Co, 1981.
8. Steinglass, P., Davis, D.I., & Berenson, D. Observations of conjointly hospitalized "alcoholic couples" during sobriety and intoxication: Implications for theory and therapy. *Family Process,* 1977, 16, 1-16.
9. Ackerman, R. *Children of Alcoholics: A Guidebook for Educators, Therapists, and Parents.* Holmes Beach, FL: Learning Publications, 1978.
10. Black, C. *It Will Never Happen to Me.* Denver: MAC Printing and Publication Division, 1982.
11. Wegscheider, S. *The Family Trap: No One Escapes from a Chemically Dependent Family.* Minneapolis: The Johnson Institute, 1976.
12. White, W.T. "Remembering children of alcoholics." Paper presented at the Annual Forum of the National Council on Alcoholism, Houston, April 1983.

13. Chafetz, M. Children of Alcoholics. *New York State University Education Quarterly*, 1979, 10, 23-29.
14. Chafetz, M.E., Blane, H.T., & Hill, M.J. Children of alcoholics: Observations in a child guidance clinic. *Quarterly Journal of Studies on Alcohol*, 1971, 32, 687-698.
15. Cork, M. *The Forgotten Children*. Toronto: Paperjacks, in association with Addiction Research Foundation, 1969.
16. el Guebaly, N., & Offord, D.R. On being the offspring of an alcoholic: An update. *Alcoholism: Clinical & Experimental Research*, 1979, 3, 148-157.
17. el Guebaly, N., & Offord D.R. The offspring of alcoholics: A critical review. *American Journal of Psychiatry*, 1977, 134, 357-365.
18. el Guebaly, N., Offord, D.R., Sullivan, K.T., & Lynch, G.W. Psychosocial adjustment of the offspring of psychiatric patients: The effect of alcoholic, depressive and schizophrenic parentage. *Canadian Psychiatric Association Journal*, 1978, 23, 281-290.
20. Moos, R., & Billings, A. Children of alcoholics during the recovery process: Alcoholic and matched control families. *Addictive Behaviors*, 1982, 7, 155-163.
21. Nylander, A. Children of alcoholic fathers. *Acta Paediatrica*, 1960, 49 suppl. 121(1), 1-34.
22. Kaminski, M., Rumeau-Roquette, C., & Schwartz, D. Alcohol consumption in pregnant women and the outcome of pregnancy. *Alcoholism: Clinical & Experimental Research*, 1978, 2, 155-163.
23. Kruse, J. Alcohol use during pregnancy. *American Family Physician*, 1984, 29, 199-203.
24. Streissguth, A.P., Barr, H.M., Martin, D.C., & Herman, C.S. Effects of maternal alcohol, nicotine, and caffeine use during pregnancy on infant mental and motor development at eight months. *Alcoholism: Clinical & Experimental Research*, 1980, 4, 152-164.
25. Behling, D.W. Alcohol abuse as encountered in 51 instances of reported child abuse. *Clinical Pediatrics*, 1979, 18, 87-91.
26. Eberle, P.A. Alcohol abusers and non-users: A discriminant analysis of differences between two subgroups of batterers. *Journal of Health & Social Behavior*, 1982, 23, 260-271.
27. Fitch, F.J., & Papantonio, A. Men who batter: Some pertinent characteristics. *Journal of Nervous & Mental Disease*, 1983, 171, 190-192.
28. Flanzer, J. Alcohol-abusing parents and their battered adolescents. In M. Galanter (Ed.), *Currents in Alcoholism*, 1979, 7, 529-538. New York: Grune & Stratton.
29. Herman, J., & Hirschman, L. Families at risk for father-daughter incest. *American Journal of Psychiatry*, 1981, 138, 967-970.
30. Mayer, J. & Black. R. The relationship between alcoholism and child abuse and neglect. In: F.A Seixas (Ed.), *Currents in Alcoholism*, 1977, 2, 429-445. New York: Grune & Stratton.
31. Orme, T.C., & Rummes, J. Alcoholism and child abuse: A review. *Journal of Studies on Alcohol*, 1981, 42, 273-287.
32. Steele, B.F., & Pollock, C.A. A psychiatric study of parents who abuse infants and small children. In: R Helfer & H Kempe (Eds.), *The Battered Child*. Chicago: University of Chicago Press, 1968.
33. Virkkunen, M. Incest offenses and alcoholism. *Medicine, Science and the Law*, 1974, 14, 124-128.
34. Sloboda, S.B. The Children of alcoholics: A neglected problem. *Hospital & Community Psychiatry*, 1974, 25, 605-606.
35. Ferguson, L., & Kirk, J. Statistical report: NIAAA-funded treatment programs, calendar year 1978. Rockville, MD: National Institute on Alcoholism and Alcohol Abuse, 1979.

36. Bohman, M. Some genetic aspects of alcoholism and criminality. *Archives of General Psychiatry,* 1978, 35, 269-276.
37. Goodwin, D.W. Biological predictors of problem drinking. In: P.M. Miller & T.D. Nirenberg (Eds.), *Prevention of Alcohol Abuse.* New York: Plenum, 1984.
38. Murray, R.M., & Stabenau, J.R. Genetic factors in alcoholism predispostion. In: E.M. Pattison & E. Kaufman (Eds.), *Encyclopedic Handbook of Alcoholism.* New York: Gardner Press, 1982.
39. Schuckit, M., Goodwin, D., & Winokur, G. A study of alcoholism in half-siblings. *American Journal of Psychiatry,* 1972, 128, 1132-1136.
40. Glynn, T.J. From family to peer: A review of transitions of influence among drug using youth. *Journal of Youth & Adolescence,* 1981, 10, 363-384.
41. Kandel, D., Kessler, R., & Margulies, R. Antecedents of adolescent initiation into stages of drug use: A developmental analysis. *Journal of Youth & Adolescence,* 1978, 7, 13-40.
42. Smart, R.G., & Fejer, D. Drug use among adolescents and their parents: Closing the generation gap in mood moderation. *Journal of Abnormal Psychology,* 1972, 79, 153-160.
43. Stanton, M.D. Drugs and the family. *Marriage & Family Review,* 1979, 2, 1-10.
44. Ziegler-Driscoll, G. The similarities in families of drug dependents and alcoholics. In: E. Kaufman & P. Kaufmann (Eds.), *Family Therapy of Drug and Alcohol Abuse.* New York: Gardner Press, 1979.
45. Goodwin, D.W., Schulsinger, F., Hermansen, L., Guze, S.B., & Winokur, G. Alcohol problems in adoptees raised apart from alcoholic biologic parents. *Archives of General Psychiatry,* 1973, 28, 238-243.
46. Goodwin, D.W., Schulsinger, F., Moller, N. Hermansen, L., Winokur, G., & Guze, S.B. Drinking problems in adopted and unadopted sons of alcoholics. *Archives of General Psychiatry,* 1974, 31, 164-169.
47. Goodwin, D.W., Schulsinger, F., Knop, J., Mednick, S., & Guze, S.B. Psychopathology in adopted and nonadopted daughters of alcoholics. *Archives of General Psychiatry,* 1977, 34, 1005-1009.
48. Cloninger, C.R., Bohman, M., & Sigardsson, S. Inheritance of alcohol abuse: Cross-fostering analysis of adopted men. *Archives of General Psychiatry,* 1981, 38, 861-868.
49. Korsten, M.A., Matsuzaki, S., Feinman, I., & Lieber, C.S. High blood acetaldehyde levels after ethanol administration: Differences between alcoholic and non-alcoholic subjects. *New England Journal of Medicine,* 1975, 292, 386-389.
50. Lindros, K.O., Stowell, A., Pikkarainen, P., & Salaspuro, M. Elevated blood acetaldehyde in alcoholics and accelerated ethanol elimination. *Pharmacological Biochemical Behavior,* 1980, 13 Suppl. 1, 119-124.
51. Truitt, E.B. Jr. Blood acetaldehyde levels after alcohol consumption by alcoholic and non-alcoholic subjects. *Advances in Mental Sciences,* 1971, 3, 212-223.
52. Schuckit, M.A., & Rayses, V. Ethanol ingestion: Differences in blood acetaldehyde concentrations in relatives of alcoholics and controls. *Science,* 1979, 203, 54-55.
53. Cohen, G., & Collins, M. Alkaloids from catecholamines in adrenal tissue: Possible role in alcoholism. *Science,* 1970, 167, 1749-1751.
54. Davis, V.E., & Walsh, M.J. Alcohol, amines and alkaloids: A possible biochemical basis for alcohol addiction. *Science,* 1970, 167, 1005-1007.
55. Blum, K. Alcohol and central nervous system peptides. *Substance & Alcohol Actions Misuse,* 1983, 4, 73-87.
56. Myers, R.D., & Melchior, C.L. Alcohol drinking: Abnormal intake caused by tetrahydropapaveroline in brain. *Science,* 1977, 196, 554-556.
57. Docter, R., Naitoh, P., & Smith, J. Electroencephalographic changes and vigilance

behavior during experimentally induced intoxication with alcoholic subjects. *Psychosomatic Medicine*, 1966, 28, 605-615.

58. Pollock, V.E., Volakva, J., Goodwin, D.W., Mednick, S.A., Gabrielli, W.F., Knop, J., & Schulsinger, F. The EEG after alcohol administration in men at risk for alcoholism. *Archives of General Psychiatry*, 1983, 40, 857-861.

59. Propping, P. Genetic control of ethanol action on the central nervous system: An EEG study in twins. *Human Genetics*, 1977, 35, 309-334.

60. Propping, P., Kruger, J., & Mark, W. Genetic disposition to alcoholism: An EEG study in alcoholics and their relatives. *Human Genetics*, 1981, 59, 51-59.

61. Porjesz, B., & Begleiter, H. Evoked brain potential deficits in alcoholism and aging. *Alcoholism: Clinical & Experimental Research*, 1982, 6, 53-63.

62. Major, L.F., & Murphy, D.L. Platelet and plasma amine oxidase activity in alcoholic individuals. *British Journal of Psychiatry*, 1978, 132, 548-554.

63. Sullivan, J.L., Stanfield, C.N., Schanberg, S., & Cavenar, J.O. Jr. Platelet monoamine oxidase and serum dopamine-beta-hydroxylase activity in chronic alcoholics. *Archives of General Psychiatry*, 1978, 35, 1209-1212.

64. Kern, J.C., Hassett, C.A., Collipp, P.J., Bridges, C., Solomon, M., & Condren, R. Children of alcoholics: Locus of control, mental age, and zinc level. *Journal of Psychiatric Treatment and Evaluation*, 1981, 3, 169-173.

65. Cantwell, D.P. Genetic studies of hyperactive children: Psychiatric illness in biologic and adopting parents. In: R.R. Fieve, D. Rosenthal, & H. Brill (Eds.), *Genetic Studies of Hyperactive Children: Psychiatric Illness in Biologic and Adopting Parents*. Baltimore, MD: Johns Hopkins University Press, 1975.

66. Goodwin, D.W., Schulsinger, F., Hermansen, L., Guze, S.B., & Winokur, G. Alcoholism and the hyperactive child syndrome. *Journal of Nervous & Mental Disease*, 1975, 160, 349-353.

67. Morrison, J.R., & Stewart, M.A. The psychiatric status of the legal families of adopted hyperactive children. *Archives of General Psychiatry*, 1973, 23, 888-891.

68. Ross, D.M., & Ross, S.A. *Hyperactivity: Current Issues, Research and Theory (Second edition)*. New York: Wiley, 1982.

69. Bohman, M. Alcoholism and crime: Studies of adoptees. *Substance and Alcohol Actions/Misuse*, 1983, 4, 137-147.

70. Cloninger, C.R., & Reich, T. Genetic heterogeneity in alcoholism and sociopathy. In: S.S. Kety, L.P. Rowland, R.L. Sidman, & S.W. Mathysse (Eds.), *Genetics of Neurological and Psychiatric Disorders*. New York: Raven Press, 1983.

71. Cloninger, C.R, Reich, T., and Wetzel, R. Alcoholism and affective disorders: Familial associations and genetic models. In: D. Goodwin and C. Erickson, (Eds.) *Alcoholism and Affective Disorders*. New York: Spectrum Publishing, 1979, pp. 57-85

72. Goodwin, D.W., Schulsinger, F., Knop, J., Mednick, S., & Guze, S.B. Alcoholism and depression in adopted-out daughters of alcoholics. *Archives of General Psychiatry*, 1977, 34, 751-755.

73. Schuckit, M. Alcoholic patients with secondary depression. *American Journal of Psychiatry*, 1983, 140(6): 711-714.

74. Williams, C.N. *Differences in Child Care Practices Among Families with Alcoholic Mothers, Alcoholic Fathers, and Two Alcoholic Parents*. Ann Arbor, Mi: University Microfilms, Inc. 1983.

75. Wegscheider, S. *Another Chance: Hope and Health for the Alcoholic Family*. Palo Alto: Science and Behavior Books, 1981.

76. Fox, R. The effect of alcoholism on children. In: *Proceedings of the 5th International Congress on Psychotherapy, Progressive Child Psychiatry*. New York: Karger, Basil, 1963.

77. Richards, T. Working with children of an alcoholic mother. *Alcohol Health and Research World*, 1979, 4(3), 22-25.

78. Ablon, J., Ames, G., & Cunningham, W. To all appearances: The ideal American family: An anthropological case study. In: E. Kaufman (Ed.), *Power to Change: Family Case Studies in the Treatment of Alcoholism.* New York: Gardner Press, 1984, pp. 199-235.

79. Peitler, E. "Comparison of the effectiveness of group counseling and Alateen on the psychological adjustment of two groups of adolescent sons of alcoholic fathers." Ph.D. dissertation, St. John University, 1980.

80. O'Gorman, P. "Self-concept, Locus of control, and perception of father in adolescents from homes with and without severe drinking problems." Ph.D. dissertation, Fordham University, 1975.

81. Herjanic, B.M, Herjanic, M., Penick, E.C., Tomelleri, C., & Armbruster, R.B.S. Children of alcoholics. In: F.A. Seixas (Ed.), *Currents in Alcoholism*, 1977, 2, 445-455. New York: Grune & Stratton.

82. Prewett, M.J., Spence, R., & Chaknis, M. Attribution of causality by children with alcoholic parents. *International Journal of the Addictions*, 1981, 16, 367-370.

83. Rouse, B.A, Waller, P.F., & Ewing, J.A. Adolescent's stress levels, coping activities, and father's drinking behavior. *Proceedings of the American Psychological Association, (81st Annual Convention)*, 1973, 681-682.

84. Liepman, M.R. Eneuresis in children of alcoholics: An epidemic. Unpublished manuscript, Ann Arbor, MI, 1977.

85. Rutter, M. *Children of Sick Parents.* London: Oxford University Press, 1966.

86. Duncan, D.F. Family stress and the initiation of adolescent drug abuse: A retrospective study. *Corrective & Social Psychiatry & Journal of Applied Behavior Therapy Methods*, 1978, 24, 111-114.

87. Gayford, J.J. Battered wives. *Medicine, Science & the Law*, 1975, 15, 237-245.

88. Hilberman, E., & Mumm, K. Sixty battered women. *Victimology*, 1978, 2, 460-470.

89. Stewart, M.A., & deBlois, C.S. Wife abuse among families attending a child psychiatry clinic. *Journal of the American Academy of Child Psychiatry*, 1981, 20, 845-862.

90. Wilson, C., & Orford, J. Children of alcoholics: Report of a preliminary study and comments on the literature. *Journal of Studies on Alcohol*, 1978, 39, 121-142.

91. Barnes, G.M. The development of adolescent drinking behavior: An evaluative review of the impact of the socialization process within the family. *Adolescence*, 1977, 12, 571-591.

92. Morehouse, E. Working in the schools with children of alcoholic parents. *Health & Social Work*, 1979, 4, 144-162.

93. Black, C. Children of alcoholics. *Alcohol Health & Research World*, 1979, 4(1), 23-27.

94. Nardi, P.M. Children of alcoholics: A role-theoretic perspective. *Journal of Social Psychology*, 1981, 115, 237-245.

95. Eldred, C.A., & Brown, B.S. Heroin addict clients' description of their families of origin. *International Journal of the Addictions*, 1974, 9, 315-320.

96. Lindbeck, V. The adjustment of adolescents to paternal alcoholism. Unpublished manuscript, Boston, 1971.

97. Cantwell, D.P. Psychiatric illness in the families of hyperactive children. *Archives of General Psychiatry*, 1972, 27, 414-417.

98. Morrison, J.R., & Stewart, M.A. A family study of the hyperactive child syndrome. *Biological Psychiatry*, 1971, 3, 189-195.

99. Stewart, M.A., deBlois, C.S., & Singer, S. Alcoholism and hyperactivity revisited: A preliminary report. In: M. Galanter (Ed.), *Currents in Alcoholism*, 1979, 5, 349-357.

100. Erickson, E. *Childhood and Society.* New York: W. W. Norton, 1950.

101. Bowlby, J. *Attachment and Loss: Volume I—Attachment.* New York: Basic Books, 1969.

102. Jahoda, G., & Cramond, J. *Children and Alcohol.* London: HMSO, 1972.

103. Tennant, F.S. Jr. Presentation at the National Drug Abuse Conference, Seattle, 1977.

104. Brooks, C. *The Secret that Everyone Knows.* San Diego: Operation Cork, 1981.

105. Carter, E.A., & McGoldrick, M. (Eds.). *The Family Life Cycle: A Framework for Family Therapy.* New York: Gardner, 1980.

106. Hartman, A., & Laird, J. (Eds.). *Family-centered Social Work Practice.* New York: The Free Press (Macmillan), 1983.

107. Smilkstein, G. The cycle of family function: A conceptual model for family medicine. *Journal of Family Practice,* 1980, 11(2), 223-232.

108. van der Hart, O. *Rituals in Psychotherapy: Transition and Continuity.* New York: Irvington Publishers, 1978.

109. Wolin, S.J., Bennett, L.A., & Noonan, D.L. Family rituals and the recurrence of alcoholism over generations. *American Journal of Psychiatry,* 1979, 136, 589-593.

110. Wolin, S.J., Bennett, L.A., Noonan, D.L., & Teitelbaum, M.A. Disrupted family rituals: A factor in the intergenerational transmission of alcoholism. *Journal of Studies on Alcohol,* 1980, 41, 199-214.

111. Gross, N., Ward, M., & McEachern, A. *Explorations in Role Analysis.* New York: Wiley, 1958.

112. Thornton, R., & Nardi, P. The dynamics of role acquisition. *American Journal of Sociology,* 1975, 80, 870-885.

113. Merton, R. The role set: Problems in sociological theory. *British Journal of Sociology,* 1957, 8, 106-120.

114. Bailey, M.B. Alcoholism in marriage: A review of research and professional literature. *Quarterly Journal of Studies on Alcohol,* 1961, 22, 81-97.

115. Price, G.M. Social casework in alcoholism. *Quarterly Journal of Studies on Alcohol,* 1958, 19: 155-163.

116. Jackson, J.K. The adjustment of the family to the crisis of alcoholism. *Quarterly Journal of Studies on Alcohol,* 1954, 15, 562-586.

117. Gorman, J.M., & Rooney, J.F. Delay in seeking help and onset of crisis among Al-Anon wives. *American Journal of Drug and Alcohol Abuse,* 1979, 6, 223-233.

118. Beckman, L.J. Women alcoholics: A review of social and psychological studies. *Journal of Studies on Alcohol,* 1975, 36, 797-824.

119. Gomberg, E.S. Alcoholism in women. In: B. Kissin & H. Begleiter (Eds.), *The Biology of Alcoholism (volume 4).* New York: Plenum Press, 1976.

120. Steinglass, P. Experimenting with family treatment approaches to alcoholism, 1950-1975: A review. *Family Process,* 1976, 15, 97-123.

121. Steinglass, P. Family therapy with alcoholics: A review. In: E. Kaufman & P. Kaufmann (Eds.), *Family Therapy of Drug and Alcohol Abuse.* New York: Gardner, 1979.

122. Liepman, M.R., Bermann, E., Cohen, H., Friedman, H., Jessup, B., Silber, S., Vazquez, J., Watson, G. Jr., Wiener, AJ., Wolper, B., Wortley, J.A., Zarkin, R. Studies of substance abusing families who abuse or neglect their children. Unpublished manuscript, Ann Arbor, MI.

123. Liepman, M.R., Doolittle, R., Nirenberg, T.D., & Broffman, T.E. (1985, October). Drinking associated family behavior: Key to relapse and recovery. Paper presented at the 43rd Annual and Second International Conference of the American Association for Marriage and Family Therapists, New York City.

124. Steinglass, P. The alcoholic family at home: Patterns of interaction in dry, wet, and transitional stages of alcoholism. *Archives of General Psychiatry,* 1981, 38, 578-84.

125. Bowen, M. Alcoholism as viewed through family systems theory and family psycho-

therapy. *Annals of the New York Academy of Science,* 1974, 233, 115-122.

126. Carter, E.A. Generation after generation: The long-term treatment of an Irish family with widespread alcoholism over multiple generations. In :P. Papp (Ed.), *Family Therapy: Full Length Case Studies.* New York: Gardner, 1977.

127. Johnson, V. *I'll Quit Tomorrow (2nd ed.).* New York: Harper & Row, 1980.

128. Koppel, F., Stimmler, L., & Perone, F. The enabler: A motivational tool in treating the alcoholic. *Social Casework: Journal of Contemporary Social Work,* 1980, 61, 577-583.

129. Minuchin, S. *Families and family therapy.* Cambridge, MA: Harvard University Press, 1974.

130. Dulfano, C. *Families, Alcoholism & Recovery: Ten Stories.* Center City, MN: Hazelden Foundation, 1982.

131. Liepman, M.R., & Nirenberg, T.D. Beginning treatment for alcohol problems. In: W. M. Cox (Ed.), *Treatment and Prevention of Alcohol Problems: A Resource Manual.* New York: Academic Press, 1986.

132. *Boylin, E. Generic encounter in the treatment of hospitalized alcoholics. American Journal of Psychotherapy,* 1980, Vol. 34 (4), 524-544.

133. Oaklander, V. *Windows to our children.* Moab, Utah: Real People Press, 1982.

134. Blume, S.B. Psychodrama and the treatment of alcoholism. In S. Zimberg, J. Wallace, & S.B. Blume (Eds.), *Practical Approaches to Alcoholism Psychotherapy.* New York: Plenum, 1978.

135. Wohl, A. & Kaufman, B. *Silent Sceams and Hidden Cries: An Interpretation of Artwork by Children from Violent Homes.* New York: Brunner/Mazel, 1985.

136. Howell, J.G. and Likorish, J.R., *Family Relations Indicator: Manual.* New York International Universities Press, 1984.

Chapter Six
Clinical Intervention with Children of Alcohol Abusers

Laura Chakrin Cable, A.C.S.W., Nora E. Noel. Ph.D., and Suzanne C. Swanson, R.N.C.,C.A.C.

Introduction

The negative impact of abusive drinking on parent-child relationships has been noted even since the times of the Old Testament. Everyone knows the story of Noah, that righteous man who saved us all from God's punishment—from the Flood. But like a shameful family secret, Noah's fate after the rainbow covenant has been less popularly told. The Scripture records that Noah was the first man to cultivate a vineyard and to get drunk. While drinking he was seen naked by his son, Ham, who thus violated his father's dignity. When Noah awoke from his stupor, he learned what had happened and cursed the descendants of Ham (1). The story is an intriguing example of the dissention related to excessive drinking —even in the best of families.

More recently, as other contributors have described, millions of Americans struggle with alcohol problems, and the children of alcohol abusers have been identified as a population at risk for medical, mental health, and substance abuse difficulties (2). Despite a wide range of individual differences and situations, they share, as a group, important common issues and a need for clinical intervention. This is not to say that every child of an alcohol abuser needs such services, but probably a significant number do.

A large percentage of these children probably never see the inside of a therapist's office (3). Their parents may never recognize their own problems with alcohol. Even if they do, the parents do not feel their child has problems severe enough to warrant treatment. For example, a parent may find it difficult to believe that a child who gets all A's in school and helps a lot around the house is in need of treatment.

In addition, the child may not want to be in treatment. An entire lifetime of keeping "the family secrets" may lead to an inability to recognize problems as being related to a parent's drinking, or to a reluctance to talk to an "outsider." Some of these issues were dealt with in an earlier chapter (4).

Within the umbrella group of children of alcohol abusers and alcoholics, there is a spectrum of children from infants to adults whose situation varies according to many factors: age, sex, culture, age of onset of parental alcohol abuse and severity of parents' drinking, presence of nonalcoholic parents, siblings, or extended family, physiological and psychological strengths and weaknesses, personality traits, ordinal position, and current family composition. Black and Wegscheider have described a range of behavior patterns in such children, from the competent, responsible ones to the troublesome family scapegoat (5,6).

Significant progress has been made in recognizing the needs of this general population (7). The next steps are to expand the types of clinical interventions available and to increase our understanding of the differential effectiveness of particular approaches. As with interventions in other areas, we would use the concept of treatment matching as a guiding principle. To rephrase Gordon Paul's classic question: What type of treatment, by whom, is the most effective and efficient for this individual, with this specific problem, and under which set of circumstances? (8).

In this chapter, our focus will be on identifying the goals and types of intervention, and on raising some of the clinical and research issues involved in treatment matching.

Need for Services: A Review of the Problem

Children of alcohol abusers, that is, offspring of any age whose parents have or have had drinking problems, may have a need for clinical intervention in two broadly defined areas: first, in the area of direct treatment services, and second, in prevention of future medical, psychological, or abuse problems.

The child may need treatment because he or she is currently

exhibiting behavioral abnormalities that can range from severe depression, anxiety, and withdrawal to violent or promiscuous acting-out. The problematic behavior patterns vary considerably as a complex function of factors previously mentioned, including the age and sex of the child, the severity of the parental alcohol problems, and the ability of the family as a whole to preserve cohesiveness and continue family rituals (9).

For example, the adult child of an alcohol abuser may first enter treatment because of problems with interpersonal relations, an inability to trust others, or an exaggerated need for control. A young child may need help because of "hyperactivity" or aggression towards other children, or may require medical treatment for problems stemming from neglect or abuse. Though the manifestations of the problems are quite different, the common issue is that these difficulties often reflect a disrupted or dysfunctional family life associated with alcohol abuse by a parental figure (10).

Because children of alcoholics are at risk for developing problems in adulthood, prevention services seem indicated despite the apparent absence of symptoms. While some children do "act out," others may appear, at least in childhood, to have adjusted quite well. They may overcompensate and become "super-achievers," doing well in school, helping around the house, being cheerful and always being ready to "lend an ear" to the parents, the rest of the family, and their many friends. These behaviors are often praised and reinforced by family, friends, and teachers, and may not be recognized as an early adaptation to an inconsistent life. Though this pattern of behavior may have been originally appropriate and useful within the child's family system, it can be inappropriate and detrimental when used in society at large. For example, an adult child of an alcoholic may find these skills useful as a member of a "helping profession," but in his personal life he may be unable to identify and satisfy his own needs (11).

Wotitz has also pointed out that though a child may appear to be functioning well within an alcoholic family system, he or she may not be able to readjust when the alcohol abuser becomes sober. "The child who has assumed the stereotypic adult role is defined by that role. When the parent returns to the family system and wants to pick up the roles that were abandoned, the child loses part of his or her identity and has no substitutes. To tell a child that you will prepare the meal and that he or she should go out and play is unfair to the child who does not know how to play. The child now feels displaced and irrelevant" (11).

The children of alcohol abusers may also be in need of prevention services because of the particularly high risk of developing their own substance-abuse problems. Results of some studies indicate that their likelihood of abusing alcohol may be up to four times more than that of the population at large (12). Current research results suggest that the high transmission rate is due to an interaction of environmental and inherited factors (9,12). Claudia Black has also suggested that children of alcohol abusers begin problematic drinking at an early age. Alcohol can provide temporary relief from the need to feel so responsible. They may believe they will never drink like their parents did, but all too often the immediate payoff is very reinforcing to the continued use and abuse of alcohol and drugs (5).

Which Services for Which Children?

Now that we and other contributors to this book have established the need for treatment and prevention services, we are faced with these questions: What kinds of services should be provided? What are the most effective and efficient interventions for children of alcohol abusers? How can these be matched with a child's particular needs?

Unfortunately, there is very little treatment outcome research with children of alcohol abusers to answer these questions. The clinical literature is replete with descriptions of various treatment and prevention protocols, and sometimes data are presented about children's recovery rates. However, the problems are different, the programs are different, and definitions and measurements of recovery are different (7). Thus, one cannot compare treatment effectiveness and efficiency across problems, programs, and populations.

Clinicians, of course, must continue to treat their patients, despite the dearth of treatment outcome research. We certainly do not advocate the position of "waiting until the results are in." Instead, we do urge clinicians to be more aware of the need for consistent data collection with accurate and objective descriptions of the patients, the problems, the methods, and the results of treatment.

On the other side of the coin, researchers should maintain awareness of the issues that the clinician must address in the treatment of alcohol abusers. In the section that follows, we will describe some treatment strategies currently used to treat children of alcohol abusers and some of the researchable issues involved in matching these methods to particular patients and problems.

Common Goals of Treatment

Almost all treatment strategies for children of alcohol abusers have nine common goals. These include: 1. assessing the children's situations and needs; 2. providing support for the children; 3. providing accurate, nonjudgmental information about alcohol, alcohol abuse, and alcoholism; 4. correcting the children's inaccurate perceptions about parental drinking problems, including helping the children to understand that the parent's inconsistent and confusing behavior is often a result of drinking, and altering their perception that they are the "cause" or reason for parental drinking; 5. helping the children to focus on their *own* behavior by giving them a sense of control over their *own* behavior and the perception of being able to make responsible choices, and if necessary, helping them learn to have fun, have friends, to feel good about themselves, and be able to concentrate on school work or job; 6. helping children learn how to cope with real situations that may arise because of the parent's alcohol abuse (for example, what to do if a parent passes out, or how to respond to a belligerent, intoxicated parent); 7. reducing the children's isolation and helping them to share their dilemma with other children in similar situations; 8. reducing the children's risk of developing substance abuse problems or, alternately, treating the children's substance abuse; 9. enlisting the family and/or other support systems to reinforce the children's gains.

Strategies for Treatment

Of the treatment strategies currently in use, a rough division can be made between those involving direct contact and those using indirect contact with the child. Direct contact methods may include (1) providing alcohol education; (2) individual counseling for the child; (3) group treatment for the child; and (4) family contact and treatment within an outpatient setting or an established treatment program for alcohol abusers. Indirect contact can include engaging both parents as partners in the modification of the child's behavior or working through the sober spouse.

Direct Methods

Alcohol Curriculum: This prevention strategy can reach the broadest numbers and can also identify those children who need more service. Schools can provide alcohol and drug education for all grades, including a psychoeducational component about how parental alcohol abuse affects families and how children tend to respond. If a climate is established that presents this in a matter-of-fact way, group participation can follow which enables children to learn how to cope with such situations. Children who are actually affected would absorb the needed information. Some of them may identify themselves and ask for more help as a result of the subject being aired. For example, the CASPAR curriculum, *Decisions about Drinking,* is a nationally known, highly successful program that also offers intensive training in its program (13,14,15).

Individual Counseling: Morehouse outlined an approach with individual children which has been implemented in school and mental health settings (16). The authors have also used these guidelines in working with children of patients in their alcohol treatment. The steps involved are identification, establishing trust, education, and counseling. During intakes with children in any setting, counselors should routinely ask about children's concerns about parental drinking. Routine screening helps to identify these concerns, which may be camouflaged by other presenting complaints.

Whether parental alcohol abuse is identified as a primary problem or one of multiple problems, it is essential for the worker to win the child's trust as someone who understands the situation. The counselor can demonstrate a matter-of-fact knowledge of the child's world by describing common experiences of children of alcoholics. For example, "I don't know if this is true for you, but lots of other kids whose parents drink too much think that it's their fault, or that their parents don't love them, or that their parents would stop if they were better kids." Of course, empathy is always essential in clinical work, but this additional outreach relieves some of the burden from the child who may not know how to verbalize his/her experience, may be inhibited by loyalty issues, and may have little reason to trust a relative stranger after numerous experiences of disappointment by adults.

Children respond to this in various ways. Some immediately agree and go on to talk in detail about their own experiences. Others acknowledge some problems but minimize their seriousness. Still others may totally deny any "negative" feelings. Counselors should provide the opportunity for children to express concerns without pressuring them. Children are naturally ambivalent about discussing their parents' problems and may need to wait until a trusting relationship has been established with the counselor. Children can also be encouraged to express their concerns in other ways, such as drawing and writing (17).

In the next step, the counselor provides alcohol education to correct any misconceptions. Education should address common issues such as blackouts, withdrawal, and how alcohol affects one's mind and body. Children often need help understanding that although Mom or Dad is responsible for doing something about the alcohol abuse, he or she did not consciously choose to become alcoholic.

Education should be responsive to the particular child's level and situation. Information can help the child accept that the parent's alcoholism does not necessarily mean a lack of love for the child. An example of the impact of education in individual counseling is how much a child's pain can be reduced when blackout is explained. The child can then better understand why the parent forgets about promises made. The child could be given books, such as Judith Seixas's *Living With a Parent Who Drinks Too Much* (18). In addition, the counselor can help the child think of "survival techniques," or specific ways to cope with problematic situations.

The next step is to help the child look at his or her own behavior with family, friends, and in school. Children's problem behaviors frequently decrease after the previous steps of intervention. However, the child may need more psychoeducational help in learning how to make friends, how to play, or how to concentrate on tasks (18,19,20).

Group Counseling: Children of alcohol abusers may be a population well-suited for group interventions, because of the benefit of learning they are not alone. Sharing situations reduces shame, isolation, and guilt, and allows the exchanging of ideas for coping with common problems. Distorted perceptions are challenged by the group's reality-testing. The structured group also gives children and adolescents success experience in relating to peers.

There have been a number of structured group programs that could be implemented at various settings. These programs generally combine techniques such as play, songs, arts and crafts, and group process to address issues including alcohol and drug information, self-esteem, and coping skills. Groups can be particularly useful for latency-aged children who are developing social skills, and for adolescents, normally occupied with peer relationships (21,22,23).

Short-term therapeutic groups can also be a vehicle for involving members in Alateen, the program for children from alcohol-troubled families that parallels the Alcoholics Anonymous program. Group leaders can help the members to overcome difficulties with children reaching Alateen, which may include the child's self-consciousness, transportation problems, and parental opposition (24). Recently, there have been some successful efforts to hold Alateen meetings at school as a way of overcoming these obstacles; workers can be involved in starting up such groups.

One important advantage of Alateen is that it enables a recovering family to participate in a shared activity. For example, on a given evening, one parent goes to an AA meeting and the other attends Al-Anon while the kids are at Alateen. Because Alateen's program is based on the same principles as AA and Al-Anon, it helps the child understand the parents' programs of recovery.

Family Intervention: In the past, most research has focused on separate alcohol abusers, spouses, or children of alcoholics, or the alcoholic couple (25).

Those studies which have claimed to explore family treatment of alcoholism have most often dealt with the couple only and have not involved the children directly in treatment. Now there is an emerging recognition of the whole family as the target of treatment (26). The clinician has the opportunity to involve the entire family when any of its members asks for assistance. Examples of the routes by which families get involved with the "helping system" include a

child referred for school-based problems, a parent being detoxi-
fied, or a nonalcoholic spouse seeking counseling.

However the family asks for help, involving the whole family in
assessment is a powerful tool in itself. This is particularly true when
done at a time of family crisis. Many alcohol-troubled families share
a tendency to set rigid boundaries with the outside world and keep
problems secret (25,26). As a system, family members adopt patterns of behavior to maintain stability of the system, with much fear
of and resistance to changing the status quo. These rigid defenses
are more permeable when the family is forced to seek outside help
during a crisis. At that time, clinicians can be firm and supportive,
bringing in all family members to explore the nature of the presenting problem and gather background information. Thus, the alcohol
abuse or alcoholism can be identified and labeled openly, paving
the way for further change.

A systematic assessment would explore family functioning,
including roles, rules, and patterns of communication within the
family. The family learns how drinking is related to these other
patterns of family life. Parents can be led to consider the impact on
children and their behavior. Other pressing family problems can be
identified, such as psychiatric or psychosocial problems. Often an
assessment reveals a serious alcohol problem which the drinker
continues to deny (27). This raises the problem of how to use the
family's leverage to intervene in an alcoholic's denial, and increase
his/her likelihood of getting treatment for the drinking. The Johnson Institute has developed a model called "Intervention" which
involves carefully coaching family and friends in supportively con-
fronting the alcoholic (28,29).

As described in previous sections, education about alcohol abuse
and alcoholism is invaluable in labeling problems that previously
caused confusion and shame. There may be particular benefits if
conducted in a multiple family group context. All members of the
family can experience a reduction in their sense of isolation, and
often it is easier to recognize what is happening in other families
than in one's own. Learning occurs through support and sharing
experiences and ways of coping.

If the alcoholic parent does acknowledge drinking as a problem
and accepts the need for rehabilitation, the family should be
involved to help maintain abstinence. During recovery, family

therapy involves reworking the family's patterns to adjust to and support the alcoholic's sobriety (30). While the family is not ultimately responsible for an alcoholic's choice to drink or stay dry, their behavior certainly influences the outcome. In addition, treatment goals go beyond abstinence and include improved family functioning in such areas as communication, marital adjustment, parenting, and social interaction.

Children may need help to understand that problems will not all automatically disappear if and when the parent stops drinking. Ironically, the child is often ambivalent about abstinence despite the hardships related to drinking. For example, the sober parent may not be as easily manipulated, and may be more strict. The child may lose gratifying functions within the family, such as being the confidante of the nonalcoholic parent (5). Finally, children may be cynical about the parents' prognosis and they may even appear antagonistic at this point if there have been cycles of abstinence and relapses in the past (19).

Relapse is a crucial issue for the family. As in individual and group counseling for children, the family must be educated about the probability of relapse and the factors that reduce the chances of relapse such as AA, disulfiram, and follow-up counseling (31). Within the family context there can be open discussion of the alcohol abusers' warning signs for building up to drinking. The family can discuss and agree on how they should respond to these warning signs, a slip, or major relapse. This agreement may help reduce the chance that family life will be totally disorganized by a return to drinking (32).

Despite planning, children are particularly vulnerable to the disappointment of relapse because they are dependent on parental functioning. Thus, they can be taught to rely on other adults such as relatives and friends and have as much ongoing support as possible even when a parent stops drinking. Possibilities include Alateen, school or church activities, and Boy Scouts and Girl Scouts. They can also be taught safety techniques to prevent emotional or physical abuse (5,19).

Indirect Methods
So far we have described modalities which involve children fully and directly. Indirect services may be indicated for several reasons: the child may resist involvement, or the parents may refuse to have

the child "exposed" to treatment. Limited resources and time may necessitate that indirect methods are the only feasible intervention. For example, many alcohol treatment programs have family workers with large caseloads who may only be able to have a few sessions with each family. Finally, indirect treatment may actually be the treatment of choice for some children of alcohol abusers.

The first two reasons are self-explanatory. The latter two require some elaboration. If the family can be seen for a limited time, the question arises as to the relative benefits of concentrating intervention on the parents, or including the whole family in sessions. This suggests an important area for evaluation research.

Children of alcoholics could be viewed as part of the larger group of children from dysfunctional or disrupted families. It is not fully known at this time if and how the behavior of children of alcoholics is different than that of children whose parents' behavior is inconsistent for other reasons such as psychiatric disorders or psychosocial stress. From the larger perspective, we can begin to borrow techniques from the literature on treating behavior disordered children.

One of the most effective methods of treating a behavior disordered child is to stop seeing the child and focusing the therapy on parents (33). In this way, the focus is shifted first from the child as an "identified patient" to the parent's relationship with the child. Then the focus is placed on the parents' relationship with each other. Seeing a child alone is sometimes an exercise in futility because the therapist is not as important to the child as his or her parents; the parents have much greater control of the child. Working with parents to improve their own relationship and better manage the child may be more effective in the long run. Modalities for indirect treatment include individual counseling for either parent, couples therapy, or multiple couples group therapy in which a variety of problems besides the alcohol abuse can be addressed, including parenting and family issues. If the alcoholic refuses treatment, the sober parent can be seen for counseling.

Treatment Matching, Questions for Further Research

Treatment for children of alcohol abusers can be conceptualized as a network of possible educational and clinical interventions including, though not restricted to, all of the modalities already described. It is important for clinicians to be flexible in formulating treatment plans for a given child and not be wed to one particular strategy; they should be able to use various interventions to complement one another.

There is a need for more research to determine which interventions or sets of interventions are most effective in producing which outcomes for which children, at what times, and delivered by whom. Are particular modalities more effective with different aged children? Is one approach more productive at a given stage in the family's adjustment to alcoholism? How does alcohol education impact a child's overall functioning? Answers to these questions should have an impact on where we choose to concentrate our treatment and training efforts.

For example, one might speculate that family therapy is more successful than group treatment with latency-aged children since transactional patterns within a family might more effectively maintain a child's behavior change. A therapeutic group may be more productive than individual counseling with teenagers since it would facilitate the developmental task of achieving peer relationships as well as addressing alcohol issues.

Jackson described stages of the family's adjustment to alcoholism (34). One wonders if widespread prevention efforts for children would enable the rest of the family to cope more quickly and constructively with parental alcoholism.

Another issue is the parental resistance to including children in treatment. What are the benefits of insisting on the entire family being involved as opposed to "staggering" treatment efforts? For example, does the alcoholic need time to achieve some stable adjustment to sobriety before being able to cope with the emotional demands of improving the marital/parental role? Does the couple need an adjustment period to strengthen their relationship before focusing on the children? Another variable is the child's willingness to engage in therapy—does the child need time to develop trust in an alcoholic parent's sobriety, or the nonalcoholic parent's determination to change?

Our own clinical experience suggests alcoholic mothers may be more resistant to having children involved in treatment than alcoholic fathers; such gender differences would be an area to explore.

Is brief family therapy effective, ineffective, or even harmful? As previously mentioned, sometimes only brief family contact is feasible due to factors such as brief hospitalization or limited staff time. Does meeting only once or twice with a family beneficially label problems and suggest possible next steps for help, or does it open a Pandora's box without sufficient time to process identified concerns? If brief contact is a "fact of life," how can we make it more effective?

Timing of interventions is an essential factor, and is related to clinicians being aware of and having access to multiple approaches. Some practical issues involve funding, insurance coverage for relatives of alcoholics, and the pragmatic issues involved in service providers networking with one another.

As we have stated earlier, clinicians must continue to treat, despite the lack of researched answers to all of our questions. We must draw on our experience, knowledge, and clients' responses to offer interventions that are as coordinated and comprehensive as possible. To illustrate the issues of timing and of using an integrated treatment approach, we present two examples of families treated by the authors at Butler Hospital:

When Mrs. A was in alcohol treatment, her husband had individual sessions and joined her for the psychoeducational Couples Group. Their three sons attended the multiple Family Group with the parents. After Mrs. A completed the three week intensive Day Hospital program, Mr. & Mrs. A. attended Couples Group for eight months, and made many adjustments to both partners' abstinence. They became more aware of behavior problems with the 10-year-old son and so as they terminated Couples Group, the parents and children entered family therapy.

When Mr. Z entered alcohol treatment his marriage was in shambles and his two daughters were highly anxious, though performing well in school. The family was seen in the Family Group, individually, and in their own family session. Because there was not enough commitment to pursue marital therapy, the follow-up plans included Mrs. Z's attending Al-Anon and individual counseling, and the daughters participating both in Alateen and a therapeutic group for children of alcoholics.

These families are just two examples of the millions that are affected by alcohol problems. As we have briefly reviewed, children of these families have a range of needs which can be addressed by prevention and treatment services. Such clinical interventions are geared at helping clients cope with the alcohol issues as well as reducing their own risk of developing psychological and/or substance abuse problems. We have outlined various modalities that can be used and we have raised a number of the researchable issues which pertain to treatment outcome and treatment matching.

References

1. Hertz, JH (ed.). *The Pentateuch and Haftorahs*. London, Soncino Press, 1981.
2. O'Gorman, P. Prevention issues involving children of alcoholics, in: *National Institute of Alcohol Abuse and Alcoholism: Services for Children of Alcoholics: Research Monograph No. 4*. Washington, DC, United States Government Printing Office, 1981.
3. Williams, K. Intervention with children of alcoholics, In: *National Institute of Alcohol Abuse and Alcoholism: Services for Children of Alcoholics: Research Monograph No. 4*. Washington, DC, United States Government Printing Office, 1981.
4. Liepman, M, Nirenberg, T, White, W. "Motivating children to participate in alcohol treatment." Paper presented at Conference on Children of Alcoholism: Clinical and Research Perspectives. Brown University, Providence, RI, March 1984.
5. Black, C. *My Dad Loves Me, My Dad Has A Disease*. California, A.C.T., 1979.
6. Wegscheider, S. *The Family Trap*. Crystal, MN, Nurturing Networks, 1976.
7. National Institute of Alcohol Abuse and Alcoholism. *Services for Children of Alcoholics: Research Monograph No. 4*. Washington, DC, United States Government Printing Office, 1981.
8. Paul, G. Behavior modification research:design tactics, in Franks, C.M. (ed.): *Behavior Therapy: Appraisal and Status*. New York, McGraw-Hill, 1969.
9. Wolin, S., Bennett, L., Noonan, D., Teitelbaum, M. Disrupted family rituals: A factor in the intergenerational transmission of alcoholism. *Journal of Studies on Alcohol* 1980; 41: 199-214.
10. Whitfield, C. Children of alcoholics: Treatment issues. In: *National Institute of Alcohol Abuse and Alcoholism: Services for Children of Alcoholics: Research Monograph No. 4*. Washington, DC, United States Government Printing Office, 1981.
11. Woititz, J. The educational aspects of serving the children of alcoholics. In: *National Institute of Alcohol Abuse and Alcoholism: Services for Children of Alcoholics: Research Monograph No. 4*. Washington, DC, United States Government Printing Office, 1981.
12. Goodwin, D., Schulsinger, F., Hermansen, L., Guze, S., Winokur, G. Alcohol problems in adoptees raised apart from biological parents. *Archives of General Psychiatry* 1973: 238-243.
13. CASPAR Alcohol Education Program. *Decisions About Drinking*. Cambridge, MA, CASPAR, 1978.

14. Deutsch, C., DiCicco, L., Mills, D. Reaching children from families with alcoholism: Some innovative techniques. *Proceedings of the Twenty-Ninth Annual Meeting of the Alcohol and Drug Problems Association of North America.* Seattle, WA, 1979.

15. DiCicco, L. Evaluating the impact of alcohol education. *Alcohol Health and Research World,* 1978; 3: 14-20.

16. Morehouse, E. Working with children of alcoholics. Presentation to the Rhode Island Symposium of the National Association of Social Workers, Newport, RI.

17. Black, C. It will never happen to me. Colorado, MAC, 1982.

18. Sexias, J. *Living With a Parent Who Drinks Too Much.* New York, Greenwillow Books, 1979.

19. Deutsch, C. Broken bottles, broken dreams. New York, Teachers College Press, 1982.

20. Woititz, J. *Adult Children of Alcoholics.* Pompano Beach, FL: Health Communications, Inc., 1982.

21. Morehouse, E. Working in the schools with children of alcoholic parents. *Health and Social Work,* 1979; 4: 144-162.

22. National Council on Alcoholism, Greater Detroit Area. *Beginning Alcohol Basic Education Studies.* Detroit, National Council on Alcoholism, 1982.

23. Hawthorne, T (ed.). *Children Are People Support Group Manual.* St. Paul, MN, Children Are People, Inc., 1980.

24. Woodside, M. *Children of Alcoholics.* New York: New York State Division of Alcoholism and Alcohol Abuse, 1982.

25. Anderson, S., Henderson, D. Family therapy in the treatment of alcoholism. *Social Work in Health Care* 1983; 3: 79-94.

26. Steinglass, P. Family therapy in alcoholism. In: Kissen, B., Begleiter, H. (eds.): *Treatment and Rehabilitation of the Chronic Alcoholic.* New York, Plenum Press, 1984.

27. Epstein, B., Bishop, D.S. Problem centered systems therapy of the family. In: Gurman, AS, Knisterh, DP (eds.): *Handbook of Family Therapy.* New York, Brunner/Mazel, 1981.

28. Johnson Institute: *Alcoholism. A Treatable Disease.* Minneapolis, MN, Johnson Institute, 1972.

29. Johnson Institute. *Intervention: A Professional's Guide.* Minneapolis, MN, Johnson Institute, 1983.

30. Meeks, D., Kelly, C. Family therapy with the families of recovering alcoholics. *Quarterly Journal of Studies on Alcohol* 1970; 31:399-413.

31. McCrady, B., Dean, L., Dubreuil, E., Swanson, S. The Problem Drinkers' Project: A programmatic application of social learning based treatment. In: Marlatt, G.A., Gordon, J. (eds.) *Relapse Prevention.* New York, Guilford Press, 1984.

32. Dean, L., Dubreuil, E., McCrady, B., Paul, C., Swanson, S. *Manual for the Butler Hospital Drinkers' Program,* Providence, RI, 1980.

33. Strauss, C., Atkeson, B. Parenting: Training mothers as behavior therapists for their children. In: Bleckman, E. (ed.) *Behavior Modification with Women.* New York: Guilford Press, 1984.

34. Jackson, J.K. The adjustment of the family to the crisis of alcohol. *Quarterly Journal of Studies on Alcohol,* 1954, 15: 562-586.

Chapter Seven
Children of Alcoholics:
One Experience at Brown*

Bruce E. Donovan, Ph.D.

As little (or as long) as ten years ago, Booz, Allen, and Hamilton noted three primary reasons why the children of alcoholic parents had attracted the attention of those interested in the prevention and treatment of alcoholism.

1. The involvement of the children can be important for the successful treatment of the alcoholic;

2. Persons who had an alcoholic parent experience a higher incidence of alcoholism than that of the general population;

3. Children of alcoholic parents are themsevles afflicted with some of the symptoms and consequences of alcoholism. No less than the alcoholic, the children suffer the effects of alcoholism (1).

Coincidental with this growing national concern with familial alcoholism was my coming to grips with my own alcoholism and that of my father and my brother, and the awareness of its risks to my own children. I could easily understand Margaret Cork's explanation of how children must be (1) taught the nature of their problems; (2) provided with a vocabulary to discuss those problems; and (3) encouraged to develop the strength to broach their secret to individuals outside the malfunctioning family unit (2).

It was comforting to learn that children of alcoholics frequently felt in some way responsible for their problem and unable to break the ethic of privacy that kept them from telling others of their plight. Further, in my own case (and in that of students I met daily) I began

---

*This paper is a revision of an earlier article, "A Collegiate Group for the Sons and Daughters of Alcoholics", *Journal of the American College Health Association*, Vol. 30, No.2, October 1981, pp. 83-86.

to observe defenses that worked splendidly, were unproblematic to others, but that nevertheless were not the result of free and conscious choice. These defenses, in fact, were behaviors which, however successful they might appear to an observer, significantly limited genuine personal development.

If these students were to initiate and sustain the personal growth that might be stimulated by awareness of their own condition, it seemed important to make special provisions for their support. When I became Associate Dean for Problems of Chemical Dependency at Brown in 1977, I realized there were not adequate supports of this nature. For many, Alateen was and continues to be of great use. For teenaged children of alcoholics to reach Alateen, however, is not always an easy matter. In the first instance its very existence is not widely known. Some have problems with the requirement of anonymity or are confused by inferences drawn from it; others balk at the spiritual focus and often misinterpret it as religious instruction.

For children of college age, who are all in a transitional stage vis-a-vis their families, Alateen, and Al-Anon also, may be problematic for another reason. Too often, as John Lavino, former director of the Personal Assistance Program of the Kemper Group, and others have noted, there is an implicit message in Al-Anon groups that maintenance of the family is of primary importance. "There is a gap in services for family members. Al-Anon and Alateen, in our experience, are inappropriate for people 18 to 25 who are single or newlyweds with no children. There are too few Alayoung groups. We hope more attention will be given by Al-Anon to the needs of this group" ... "We believe the unspoken and unwritten premise of many Al-Anon groups is 'keep the family together at all costs.' We would like to see Al-Anon and its members talk more about the health of the individual family member(s) and then talk about whether or not the marriage or family can stay intact" (3). This orientation can be inhibiting for college-age children who in the best of situations may not return to live with family, and is surely problematic for those who have yearned for a long time to disassociate themselves from family. Most agreeably, members of Al-Anon themselves have sensed this difficulty and have now adopted procedures and literature that focus specifically on the problems of adult children of alcoholics.

However, in 1979, to meet the needs of sons and daughters of alcoholics, I felt compelled to devise a special group to provide information and orientation, support in moments of acute crisis, and a network of individuals with similar backgrounds who would be available to one another for ongoing support.

A mailing went out to approximately twenty students whom I had come to know directly or through referrals from peer counselors, friends, parents, faculty, the Health Service, and the chaplains. The mailing announced formation of a group that would address questions faced by children of alcoholics. The group would assume an alcoholic parent for each participant and would not focus directly on the issue of the parent's illness. Rather, the group was to consider those feelings and responses learned in dealing with the home situation that might appear in dealings with other individuals in other settings. Examples cited included inordinate feelings of responsibility, anger, helplessness, guilt, distrust, low self-confidence, and worry about security. Difficulties in dealing with authority were also mentioned. It was stated that light background reading would be required. Strict confidence was essential.

A month later, a follow-up mailing went out. Nine students indicated interest in the project and formed a group. (Let me note that students were in every instance allowed to ignore my overtures.) Despite the range in ages, backgrounds, and familiarity with the problems of alcoholism, the group was congenial and very tolerant of one another. Sketches of the participants are given at the end of the chapter. Each session was held in a pleasantly furnished, non-institutional lounge on campus. Light refreshments were served to promote a relaxed and informal atmosphere. The sessions were simple in design. As facilitator, I tried to remain unobtrusive, but I shared my own history as appropriate.

The first meeting was devoted to explanation of the group's rules and purposes. Confidentiality was stressed. Students were reminded that each member of the group had at least one alcoholic parent, that this was a credential for attendance, and that there would be no disinterested spectators present. Honesty was emphasized, as was the need for mutual trust. An important operating rule emerged: Students must speak only of their own experiences and had to use "I" statements throughout. No one was to be forced even implicitly to speak; silence, theoretically, was a permissible option for everyone. Students were encouraged to empathize as fully as they might, seeking points of identification rather than of distinction. Advice-giving was to be avoided, as was probing for details that a participant might not readily share. The goal was a warmly supportive environment in which one's statements might be challenged, but only gently. It was stressed often that group members might be articulating for the first time feelings and ideas that they had never shared: sensitivity was vital. Emphasis was always placed on the idea that life is not a random proposition, that we can all learn to choose patterns for our own futures, and that these patterns need not be those we grew up with.

Each student was asked to identify himself or herself in terms of alcoholic parentage and background. Some spoke at length, others sparingly. Conversation was so easy that plans were abbreviated for a full review of "the Jellinek Curve", a schematic representation of the progression of alcoholism. Participants were given a copy of "the Curve" and a copy of Cork's "Forgotten Children". (This assignment was made too early. Students found it "heavy stuff," difficult to read, and remarked that "it made me squirm" and was "too familiar").

At the second session a short talk on the effects of alcoholism in the family was planned. (At this session attendance was very low —three out of nine—but the group continued.)The third session, fully attended, was devoted to a consideration of Wegscheider's scheme for roles assumed by members of an alcoholic family as outlined in her pamphlet, The Family Trap (4). Particular emphasis was put on the role of "the lost child". Participants were asked to identify aspects of the roles which meshed with their own experiences.

The fourth session was devoted to the viewing of the film "If You Loved Me." The film unlocked sensitivity and awareness. Conversation after the viewing was initially slow, but picked up; not surprisingly, conversation focused on the aesthetic aspects of the film and later moved on to the more painful issues of the alcoholic family.

The fifth session reverted to Wegscheider's typology and specifically to "the family hero." One student remarked that he "never felt as much like others before." The role of the hero in the highly competitive atmosphere at Brown was very familiar and helped students understand who they were. It was important in this discussion to clarify that the achievements of the "heroic child" were in themselves laudable, that motivation and incentives—not achievement—were the concern. To achieve and overachieve as compensatory behavior is perhaps to achieve for improper motives.

The sixth session was held in my home with my wife, a nonalcoholic, in attendance. The format was a potluck supper, a format chosen to insure group participation and to heighten feelings of mutual friendship and dependability. The event was judged a great success. Conversation was wide-ranging and focused on Wegscheider's role of "the enabler". Students seemed particularly interested in my wife's experience and observed with fascination the awkwardness for us both in answering their questions.

Students were asked to evaluate the group, both verbally and through written questionnaires. All eight students who responded judged their experience positively. In two questions that targeted their expectations, students explained that their expectations generally centered on the ability to understand present behavior in the context of past experiences and the desire for an opportunity to talk with people in a similar situation. Six remarked that the expectations had been met to one extent or another.

Seven of the eight respondents answered that there were issues that they wish had been explored. Some of these issues were cognitive (for example, the legal rights of the children of alcoholics), and several remarked on specific problems such as self-esteem, trust, and relationships outside the family. One student wrote: "It's hard to say. The more I learn about alcoholism, the more issues come up."

When asked whether new information had been acquired, students cited insights into their personal involvement, their reactions to their familial alcohol problem, and the dynamics of the alcoholic family. Others mentioned a new awareness of the prevalence of the alcoholic family. All eight students responded that they acquired new feelings in the group. These emotional insights included anger, trust, and increased self-esteem. The abundance and variety of responses on this inventory of new emotional reactions suggests the potential effectiveness of the group and the need to refer students (as appropriate) to other, more sustained counseling.

When asked if they had found unexpected "pluses," all eight students checked an affirmative response. Their benefits chiefly centered on the acquisition of new friends and confidants and the discovery of new support from the group. One student remarked that he "enjoyed sharing and learning from people who have played against the same team." Several remarked the value they experienced in encountering a "pleased smile and spirited 'hi'" (from a group member on campus) and that "running into group members when they are smiling is always a pleasure and reassuring." One student spoke perhaps for others in the group: "There seems to be a special bond that maybe I don't deserve, but it's there and I treasure it. We all see each other as we are. I've been able to accept and give support as I have been unable to before. A new family? Maybe." This last comment is a moving testimony to the potential effectiveness of a very simple group.

What general observations might I make on the effectiveness of the group? The providing of new information was easily achieved and worthwhile; as straightforward instruction, this task was clearly worth the effort. Later contacts with some individuals in the group allow me to say that the information was retained and proved useful well after the last session. This fact has implications, surely, for evaluation. The establishment of an informal network of kindred souls was helpful for the students, economical for the institution, of relief and assistance to the facilitator. The new sense of freedom experienced by group members seemed real and was surely gratifying.

More can be done by more individuals to deal with this population. The literature suggests that problems common to children of alcoholics are shared by other children (for example, children of incest and other abusive situations, children of Holocaust survivors). With little additional orientation, those trained to deal with these other issues could deal effectively with children of alcoholics. Also, the realization that others bear scars from their parents' behavior is a helpful antidote to the feeling among children of alcoholics of their uniqueness in "unfairly" have to "pay" for parental activity. More discussion of the drinking habits of children of alcoholics — in general and with reference to group members — would have been welcome.

The purposes of groups such as this should embrace children

affected by parental use of drugs other than alcohol. It was an error to continue the group in almost casual fashion with highly irregular attendance. A monthly reunion would have been preferable, if there were desire to continue the group. As it was, the group never achieved full closure. Great difficulty and anxiety seemed to center on the on-again, off-again nature of the group's meetings. Some members observed that the uncertainty of this process provoked responses similar to those used in dealing with their malfunctioning families. This observation should suggest dissatisfaction only with a troublesome closure and not failure of the group experience as a whole.

My own alcoholism perhaps helped the group, as did the fact of my own alcoholic parentage. Such personal involvement is not necessary, however. From an institutional prespective the existence of the group (with the publicity attendant upon it) has helped sensitize some members of the Brown community to the prevalence and extent of alcohol-related problems on campus. I also note with gratification that Brown has served (in this area as in others) as a model for similar groups on other campuses. Happily, Brown students now have on-campus access at present to three Al-Anon groups—one traditional, another made up primarily of undergraduates, and a third devoted to adult children of alcoholics. A group for children of alcoholics also continues to be offered outside the anonymous movements.

Sketches of group participants follow. Although these biographies are created from true details, they have been rearranged with changes in such telling characteristics as names of cities and occupations to protect the privacy of actual group participants. Not all students participated in the group at one time.

Earl was the enormously energetic son of the general counsel of a major firm based in Chicago. His father had been sober for four years. Earl was not eager to raise the issues with his father but wanted to gain insight, it developed, into dynamics between his father and mother.

Martha was the Asian-American daughter of an unemployed, active alcoholic whose appearance was so disreputable that he was reported as a vagrant in the dorm when he came to visit his daughter. Martha was also heavily involved romantically with an Antabuse-maintained senior male.

Lisa was the athletic daughter of an abusive, active alcoholic father. Lisa and her siblings were regarded as "pigs" by their father and were regularly forced to consume gross amounts of bacon and gallons of ice cream. Her self-esteem was almost nonexistent.

Kathy had come to me as a sophomore when she was serving as a resident counselor to freshmen; she was concerned about excessive drinking on the hall. She mentioned her father's alcoholism at that time. We discussed it briefly. Kathy was not directly concerned about it until her senior year.

Louis was a Black junior plagued by nocturnal calls from his mother who was an active alcoholic who discussed suicide routinely.

Madge had been angry for years over the neglect shown her by her actively alcoholic father, whom she loved deeply. She was troubled by her romantic fascination with older men. Her father died while she was participating in the group.

Rick was the son of an actively alcoholic mother whose drinking surfaced as a professional liability for Rick's father, a corporate executive whose business entertaining had to be seriously curtailed.

Brett was the son of a sober father and an actively dually-addicted mother. Brett was concerned about his own relationship with his parents, with financial matters, and with the plight of his three younger siblings.

Laura was the daughter of an actively alcoholic father, who had recently been divorced by Laura's mother. Laura's father came to sobriety during the course of the group.

Todd was the academically successful son of a glamourous Denver socialite who was actively alcoholic. Todd was concerned about his inability to discuss the issue with his mother (to whom he was devoted), even when the issue was injected through her actions directly into their relationship.

Lena and Brad were the children of a divorced couple. Their father was an active alcoholic who was dying of cancer. Lena, who chose to discuss the issue, was troubled because she did not feel badly about her father's imminent death and was almost happy about it. Brad was a junior, Phi Beta Kappa, and was accepted (ultimately) into some of the best graduate schools in the nation. He was not interested in discussing the issue.

References

1. Booz, Allen, and Hamilton: An assessment of the Needs of and Resources for Children of Alcoholic Parents: A Report Prepared for the National Institute for Alcohol Abuse and Alcoholism, (Contract #ADM41-74-0017, Modification #1), November 30, 1974.
2. Cork, M: *The Forgotten Children.* Paperjacks, in association with the Addiction Research Foundation, 1969.
3. Lavino, J: *"Family Members of Alcoholics in the Workplace: Al-Anon as Treatment Resource,"* unpublished transcript of a paper presented at the Annual Forum of the National Council on Alcoholism, Seattle, 1980.
4. Wegscheider, S: *The Family Trap.* Minneapolis: Nurturing Networks, 1979.

PROVIDING CARE (90)

Chapter Eight
The Connection Between Alcoholism, Child Maltreatment, & Family Disruption

Carol N. Williams, Ph.D. and Edward W. Collins, M.D.

Almost universally, descriptions of children being beaten, burned, or neglected by their parents provoke strong feelings in members of our society. We find these practices abhorrent. From a historical perspective, however, this was not always so. Recognition of children's rights and some balance between the rights of parents and rights of children are recent developments. A historical review of this evolution will provide us with a better understanding of current child abuse problems, the roots of our reluctance to address them, and the relationship between child abuse and alcoholism.

History

Infanticide, the purposeful murder of an infant child by the parent, would by today's standards be defined as an extreme form of child abuse subject to criminal prosecution. But in the past, this was a common and condoned legal practice. In the *Code of Hammurabi,* which dates back to 2150 BC, the first written statement of the principle of *Patria Potestas,* (the father as absolute) is found. Here, parents are given broad latitude for what they may do with the child, including homicide. The Code also states that any child who raises a hand against the parent will have that hand cut off (1).

In the *Hebrew Code* around 600 BC the concept of parental absolutism is preserved. Children are considered to be chattels of the father until he dies. In pre-Christian Rome around 500 BC the

Law of the Twelve Tablets gave guidance as to which children should be allowed to survive. Those with handicapping conditions or whose birth overextends the family's resources could, with the permission of the state, be put to death.

Despite the prevailing lack of children's rights, a few bright spots existed for children. The Jewish Passover, where great efforts were made to save the first born against the threats of the state, is an excellent example of a change in attitudes toward children. Similarly, the Coming of the Christ Child represented acknowledgment of the value of a child and perhaps contributed to some change in attitude. But for the most part, the practices of extremes in discipline, selling into slavery, and infanticide continued.

It was not until the 1300s and 1400s in English Common Law that children were recognized as having any rights at all. Through the law they were allowed to inherit property and wealth. Moreover, individuals outside the family could be appointed guardian ad litums and represent the child's interest in court proceedings, a practice that continues today.

Abandonment was to replace infanticide as the most common way to dispose of unwanted children in the 1400s and 1500s. The first foundling hospital was established in Italy in the 1420s to cope with this problem. A profound change in the conceptualization of childhood began to occur among philosophers and writers in the 1600s and 1700s. Previously, children had been regarded as little adults but the idea of childhood as a special time began slowly to develop. Rousseau wrote in *Emile*, "Children should be children before they are men," and John Locke proposed that the purpose of childhood was to learn the skills necessary to become appropriate and successful adults.

While today we have little trouble accepting these views, at the time these ideas were revolutionary and ran deeply against the grain of prevailing beliefs. Extremes of physical punishment were justified by biblical quotations of "If thou smite him with a rod do deliver him from hell," or more popularly, "Spare the rod and spoil the child." These beliefs were brought to Colonial America. In 1628 members of the Massachusetts Bay Colony wrote the Massachusetts Stubborn Child Act into their law. It stated that any male child of sufficient age, about 16, who failed to respond to his parent's direction could, with the approval of the State, be put to death.

With the Industrial Revolution, a shift from an agrarian to an industrial society occurred with a corresponding shift in types of tasks children were expected to accomplish. Many of their farm tasks had been more appropriate to their abilities than were industrial tasks which pushed them beyond their limits and increased their proneness to illness and injury. The plight of these children is well portrayed in the novels of Charles Dickens. In England almost all chimney sweeps were children who were deliberately underfed to allow them to fit through narrow flues. However, the Industrial Revolution also produced a new middle class with concerns about quality of life and a willingness to accept the philosophers' concepts about the value of childhood. Things were changing for children, but not quickly.

In the United States, children's rights were not a legal concern until the famous 1874 case of Mary Ellen, one of many abandoned children in New York City who had been placed in a proprietary foster home. Reports of her ill-treatment came to the attention of a church group which reported the incidents to the police. The reply was that, sad as the case may be, no laws existed that defined child maltreatment as an offense, and they could do nothing. The case was taken to court and testimony provided by a representative of the Society for the Prevention of Cruelty to Animals. Based on this testimony, the judge ruled in favor of the child and removed her from the home. The American Society for the Prevention of Cruelty to Children was formed the next year and remains active in many states today.

However, children's rights advocates made very few gains over the next decades and the concept of parental absolutism continued until the 1950s. Then in 1962 Henry Kempe (2) wrote a classic article on "The Battered Child Syndrome" in which he described deliberate infliction of injuries by parents on children. Moreover, he devoted the remainder of his career to raising society's awareness about the maltreatment of children. It was an idea whose time had come and in the 1960s and 1970s every state in the union passed statutes that recognized child abuse and gave the state broad *parens patraie* (state as parent) rights to intervene into a family in the interest of a child to protect him or her from further harm.

The statutes recognized four types of child maltreatment: physical abuse by the caretaker; neglect of nurture and nourishment;

emotional abuse; and sexual abuse. States were given the right to remove children from the home when needed and laws were passed in many states legally obligating anyone with knowledge of child abuse or neglect to report such cases to the state. Child protective services were established to investigate these reports and manage the cases. Most state statutes also affirmed the traditional values of family by stating that all attempts be made to reunite the child with his or her family as soon as possible. These statutes supported the child protective agencies' responsibility for building their own programs of remediation in addition to investigation and management of cases.

There are really two components of child abuse management: the legal and the social. Legal definitions of child abuse are quite specific and the basic test is that the injury or condition observed in the child be non-accidental and caused usually by the actions of a parent. The social definitions are not as clear. Based on the concept of childhood as a special time with special rights to health and happiness, a useful social definition of child abuse is "any interaction or lack of interaction that causes physical or developmental harm"(3, pp.251-2). Because this definition can include emotional neglect or verbal abuse which are not always directly observable or consistently defined even by experts, this broad definition is not easily tested legally. The social definition of child abuse is especially relevant when considering the impact of alcoholism on family functioning and children's physical and emotional development.

Connection Between Alcohol Use and Child Abuse

The actual prevalence of child abuse in the general population is unknown. Various estimates of incidence of child abuse and neglect range from 500,000 to 1,000,000 cases a year and are fairly equally divided between reports of abuse and of neglect (4). The United States leads the Western world in cases of fatal child abuse for children under the age of four, with the number being greatest for those less than one year of age. However, abuse and neglect can occur throughout the child's life. Girls may be more likely to be abused and boys to be neglected . Income is not as important an indicator as was once thought.

Consensus is lacking among professionals as to the extent of the connection between alcoholism and child abuse. Estimates of abuse and neglect vary widely, depending on what kind of study is conducted. The difficulties in establishing an association between alcohol use and child abuse stem from the fact that terms are inadequately defined, specification of alcohol use at the time of the incident is often lacking, clinical samples are frequently small and biased, and the studies rely heavily on therapist impression, personal reports, and case records.

In general, national epidemiological studies of child abuse and neglect report lower percentages of alcohol involvement at the time of the incident than do clinically-based samples of abused children. In a national study of 1,380 occurrences of child abuse, Gil reported that 13% of the parents were intoxicated at the time of the incident (5). Out of 18,277 validated cases of abuse and neglect, the American Humane Association linked almost 17% of the cases to alcohol dependence (6). In a hospital-based sample, however, Collins and the child protection team found that 33% of their cases involved alcohol abuse by the caretaker (7).

When samples of alcoholic parents are studied for concurrent child abuse and neglect, the reported statistics are also higher than those reported in epidemiological studies. Black and Mayer (8) intensively studied the child care practices of 92 alcoholic and 108 opiate-addicted parents who were in a detoxification unit. Based on parental reports, all the children in these families were judged to be mildly neglected. Physical abuse occurred in 27% of the alcoholic families and 19% of the opiate-addicted families. Serious neglect occurred in 28% of the alcoholic families and 32% of the opiate-addicted families.

Although 48% of these parents had been abused as children, they made a conscious effort not to abuse their own children. Those parents who were abusive often came from disrupted homes and had been abused by their own problem drinking parents . This intergenerational link between abusive and neglectful parenting and alcohol problems was also found by Behling (9), who reported that in 51 cases of reported child abuse at a military base, 69% of the cases had at least one alcohol-abusing parent and 63% of the cases had an alcohol-abusing grandparent. Most of the parents who themselves had been abused as children had an alcoholic parent.

In order to explore whether the differences in incidence of abuse and neglect were associated with the gender of the alcoholic parent, Williams (10) compared the child care practices of three groups of alcoholic parents: both alcoholic, mother only, and father only. Families with two alcoholic parents displayed the highest percentage of abuse and neglect, the most inconsistent discipline (their children had the highest number of both hits and hugs), the most medical problems at childbirth, and the least positive attitude toward their children of the three parent groups. These parents were also significantly younger and had the most serious drinking problems of the three groups.

The alcoholic mothers group showed the lowest social and economic stability of all the parents. Three-fourths had been left by their mates. They functioned better than the two alcoholic parent groups, but not as well as the alcoholic father group. Their children were most likely to be neglected but not abused. The mothers seemed overwhelmed financially, and isolated socially.

The families with alcoholic fathers had the greatest economic, social and marital stability, the most adequate child care, and most positive attitude toward their children of the three groups. However, these men all had a non-problem drinking wife in the home to care for the children. Compared to families without alcoholism, however, the functioning of these fathers' families was still below average. In conclusion, it would appear that children are at differential risk for abuse and neglect in alcoholic families, depending on which parents are alcoholic, and this differential should be taken into account when assessing the impact of familial alcoholism on the children.

It is difficult to assess the relationship between alcoholism and sexual abuse, but it is believed to occur at an increased rate among children of alcoholics. For instance, in one survey of 200 adult children of alcoholics, 30% of the women reported the presence of incest in their childhood (11). Barnard (12) speculates that the occurrence of incest and alcohol abuse in the same families may be quite high, because the same family dynamics of shame, guilt, denial, and silence operate in both situations. In summary, clinical samples of alcoholics and child abuse cases would lead one to believe that an association between alcohol abuse and physical abuse and neglect exists among approximately 30% of the cases.

More needs to be known about this relationship in order to develop more effective intervention strategies.

Effects of Alcoholism on Family Functioning

It is much more difficult to calculate the impact of alcoholism on family functioning and the child's development when these effects are not manifest in terms of documentable physical neglect or abuse. Emotional neglect and abuse (defined as inappropriate and extreme verbal assaults and blame against children for situations beyond their control), are hard to identify and measure. We know that in order to develop into healthy, well-adjusted adults, children must have their physical needs for food, shelter, clothing and medical care, and their emotional needs for attention, love, and self-esteem met. They need stability and consistency in their home life and development of security and trust that their dependency needs will be met. Yet, in general, the homes in which children of alcoholics grow up are unstable financially and emotionally, inconsistent and unreliable in child care, and lacking in close relationships between parent and child. The developmental outcomes for these children are often personality difficulties, inadequate coping skills, and drinking or other drug abuse problems, as well as impaired parenting ability with their own children.

Several studies illustrate the extent of the disruption that occurs in alcoholic families, even with the socio-economic status controlled. In a French study of children in a child psychiatry clinic, twice as many children of alcoholics had divorced parents as children from families without alcoholism, the court had to intervene into family violence nine times more often in homes with alcoholism, and a third of these children were permanently removed from their homes (13). A 20-year longitudinal study by Miller and Jang (14), in which low income alcoholic families in Oakland were matched to families without alcoholism from the same neighborhood, 68% of the children of alcoholics came from broken or unstable homes, and 39% were removed by social agencies, as compared to 25% and 19% respectively of children from the non-alcoholic homes.

Even with upper and middle income alcoholic women, 39% of the mothers interviewed in one study were maritally separated for long periods of time, and 20% of their children were raised by someone else (15). Another study of higher income alcoholic mothers' attitudes toward their children found them to be ambivalent and confused in their relationships with their children (16). They were alternately rejecting and overprotective of the children, and inconsistently strong disciplinarians. The adequacy of child care in all these families is of crucial importance, yet, too often, it is unaddressed by clinicians and researchers alike.

One of the ways that children of alcoholics manifest their anxiety is through physical ailments. These children experience more illnesses and accidents than do other children. One adolescent health clinic reported that teenagers, particularly girls, identified as having problem drinking parents, also displayed twice the number of somatic complaints as teenagers without identified problem drinking parents (17). In another study, researchers randomly sampled a general teenage population and found that those children who perceived their fathers to be heavy drinkers also demonstrated greater physical and psychological stress than did youths who did not report heavy drinking by their fathers (18). Clinicians in health settings need to be sensitive to these indicators in order to respond to these nonverbal cries for help.

What do the children themselves say about all this? *The Forgotten Children*, by Margaret Cork (19), is one of the most moving descriptive studies available for presenting the child's perspective of life in alcoholic families. It was the emotional neglect and family conflict that most upset the children, not the drinking *per se*. Parental quarrels, fear of divorce, and inconsistent discipline bothered them. They felt rejected, unloved and resentful at having to assume many parental responsibilities to keep the family functioning. The children were "constantly angry" at both parents, the nondrinking spouse as well as the drinking one. These feelings remained surprisingly strong into adulthood, and adult children of alcoholics expressed greater difficulty with issues of trust, intimacy, sexuality, and interpersonal relationships (20) than youth from nonalcoholic homes. Young females were especially hurt by the feelings of being unloved and would seek affection outside the home, often through sexual relationships and at a younger age than their peers.

The emotional neglect, abuse and disruption in families with alcoholism is devastating to the children. Professionals must be able to recognize and intervene into these situations for the welfare of the child and the health of the family as a whole. It is not enough to engage the alcoholic in alcoholism counseling, or even both spouses into couples counseling. The children already have many painful memories and misconceptions about themselves, their families, and life in general that must be expressed and postively reconstructed with professional help for the children's future health. Long-term therapy is not necessary in many cases. Educational groups that address alcoholism, its effect on the child and family, coping strategies, and affirmation of the child's feelings and self-esteem can be quite effective for increasing the child's sense of well-being.

Correlates of Abuse

Identifying the presence of situations in which emotional neglect and abuse are present is admittedly difficult. This difficulty is increased by reluctance to intervene into "personal" matters, such as drinking or "family" matters such as abuse, due to the historic concept that, "A man's home is his castle," and what happens within it is no one else's business. However, societal thinking is becoming more egalitarian in terms of the rights of children (and wives), to protection from dangerous family situations, and intervention into these situations is more acceptable. In order to help service providers recognize potentially dangerous situations for children, some warning signs that should alert clinicians and counselors to the possibility of abuse and neglect are as follows:

Caretaker Characteristics
1. Parental history of abuse in childhood
2. Birth complications or unwanted pregnancy
3. Young, inexperienced parents (teens and early twenties,
4. Single parents with no lifeline or support network
5. Domestic violence
6. Frequent contact with social services
7. Substance abuse
8. Job loss
9. Unrealistic expectations of the child
10. Inconsistency in discipline, complaints about the child's behavior

Child Characteristics

1. Fatal abuse more likely for infants and under one year of age
2. Girls more likely to be abused, boys to be neglected
3. School or behavior problems—changes in behavior
4. Behavior extremes of aggressiveness, shyness, fearfulness
5. Greater frequency of accidents or illnesses, especially psycho-somatic ones.
6. Unusual bruises, marks, reluctance to discuss them
7. Physical appearance, hygiene not adequate

Professionals do have alternatives available to them if they suspect alcoholism and child abuse or neglect. Most states have a child abuse hotline that protects the caller's anonymity and will investigate a report, even if only a suspicion of abuse is evident. Large hospitals with pediatric units usually have child protection teams which will provide consultation, as do most mental health clinics. Parents can be referred to Alcoholics Anonymous and Parents Anonymous, which are free, self-help groups widely accessible, or to private counseling. Children can be referred for counseling and to special groups for abused children and for children of alcoholics. Alateen is another resource for children of alcoholics. On an individual basis, just being a friend and someone to be trusted can be extremely important to a child's development and help mitigate some of the negative effects of the family.

In order to break the intergenerational cycle of alcoholism and of physical, emotional, and sexual abuse, and to ameliorate their negative effects on the child, professionals need to screen more aggressively for possible alcoholism and child abuse and neglect in families, and then intervene. Health care professionals need to learn about alcoholism, alcoholism counselors need to delineate more clearly the connection between alcohol use and child maltreatment, and make the implications of this research available to clinicians and policy-makers.

More training and greater cooperation and interchange of knowledge among professionals in different disciplines is needed. The reason for anyone's reluctance to intervene into a family is evident from the history given at the beginning of this chapter, but to do nothing is to become a participant in the process of child maltreatment. In this society, we do have a responsibility to be advocates and protectors of the children, and we must have the courage to act upon this responsibility.

References and Notes

1. Robin, M. Historical introduction-sheltering arms: The roots of child protection. In: E.H. Neuberger (ed), *Child Abuse*. Boston: Little, Brown, & Co., 1982. THe history in this section can be found in this chapter.
2. Kempe, C. H., Silverman, F.N., Steele, B.F., Droegemuller, W. & Silver, H.K. The battered child syndrome. *Journal of the American Medical Association*, 1962, 181 (17).
3. Helfer, R.E., A review of the literature of the prevention of child abuse and neglect. *Child Abuse and Neglect*, 1982, Vol. 6, pp. 251-253.
4. National Study of the Incidence and Severity of Child Abuse and Neglect, DHHS Publication Number 81-30329 (OHDS), 1981.
5. Gil, D. *Violence Against Children*. Cambridge, MA: Harvard University, 1970.
6. American Humane Society. *National analysis of official child abuse and neglect reporting*. Denver, Colo: Author, 1978.
7. Personal communication by the author, March 2, 1984.
8. Black, R. & Mayer, J. Parents with special problems: Alcoholism and opiate addiction. *Child Abuse and Neglect*, 1980, 4, 45-54.
9. Behling, D.W. Alcohol abuse as encountered in 51 cases of child abuse. *Clinical Pediatrics*, 1979, 18, 87-88, 90-91.
10. Williams, C.N. *Differences in Child Care Practices Among Families with Alcoholic Fathers, Alcoholic Mothers, and Two Alcoholic Parents*. Ann Arbor, Mi: University Microfilms, 1982.
11. Forrest, G.G. Many children of alcoholics overcome difficulties. *U.S. Journal*, March 1981, 5(3), 6.
12. Barnard, C.P. Alcoholism and incest part 1: Similar traits, common dynamics. *Focus on the Family and Chemical Dependency*, 1984, 7(1), 27-34.
13. Bourgeois, M., Levigneron, M. & Delage, H. The children of alcoholics: A study of 66 children of alcoholics in a child psychiatry clinic. *Annales Medico-Psychologiques*, 1975, 2(3), 592-609. (Translated by NCALI).
14. Miller, D. & Jang, M. Children of alcoholics: A 20 year longitudinal study. *Social Work Research and Abstracts*, 1977, 13(4), 23-29.
15. Corrigan, E.M. *Alcoholic Women in Treatment*. New York: Oxford University Press, 1980.
16. Krauthamer, C. Maternal attitudes of alcoholic and nonalcoholic upper middle class women. *International Journal of the Addictions*, 1979, 34, 639-644.
17. Biek, J.E. Screening test for identifying adolescents adversely affected by a parental drinking problem. *Journal of Adolescent Health Care*, 1981, 2, 107-113.
18. Rouse, B.A., Waller, P.F., & Ewing, J.A. Adolescent stress levels, coping activities, and father's drinking behavior. In Proceedings of the American Psychological Association, 81st Annual Convention, 1973, 681-682.
19. Cork, M. *The Forgotten Children: A Study of Children with Alcoholic Parents*. Toronto, Canada: Paperjacks, 1969.
20. Booz-Allen & Hamilton. An assessment of the needs of and resources for children of alcoholic parents. (Report commissioned by NIAAA) Rockville, Md., National Institute on Alcohol Abuse and Alcoholism, 1974.

Chapter Nine
Children of Alcoholic Parents:
Public Policy Issues

Sheila B. Blume, M.D.

Other chapters in this book have painted a picture of the children of alcoholic parents as a population at risk for a wide range of alcohol, drug abuse, mental health and social problems. They have also described a population in pain, one that suffers in isolation the insecurity, anxiety, and shame of a "family secret" that cannot be shared. These children have been described as an important target for help, both as individuals and in schools, universities, clinics, professional practices, and institutional settings.

In this chapter, however, we will consider children of alcoholics on a different level: that of public policy. Policy considerations require a very different approach from that appropriate to considerations of therapy for the suffering individual. Well-meaning policies can be harmful. Ethical considerations abound, and must balance the rights, responsibilities, and interests of the child, the parent, the family unit, and society.

In September, 1983, the *American Medical News,* the newsletter of the American Medical Association, printed a letter from a member who responded to an article about bringing help to alcoholic and drug-addicted physicians (1). The writer suggested that prevention made more sense than treatment, and since the "preponderance of available studies suggest the drug/alcohol abuser's family of origin as the likely source of addictive behavior, regardless of the drug," he proposed that "preventing an already drug-dependent or predisposed future physician from entering the ranks would save lots of time, money, liability and bad press for the profession as a whole."

The argument may sound reasonable on the surface (i.e., choosing prevention rather than treatment), but the author is actually proposing that the children of alcoholic parents be disqualified from entering the field of medicine simply on the basis of family history. He proposes this in the name of rational public policy. If these people are to be excluded from medicine, why not also from law, aerospace, driving, psychology, the Congress, the clergy and the presidency? One can imagine the screening process and the effect it would have in deterring parents from seeking treatment, and in deterring doctors from making accurate diagnoses. Such a proposal is an excellent example of the mischief that can be perpetrated in the name of being helpful. It is also an example of the many different judgments involved in policy formation. This chapter will review some of the questions of social policy that are of special relevance to children of alcoholic parents, with the hope of stimulating careful consideration, discussion, and in some cases, social action.

School-based Programs

Labeling and confidentiality. The child who is offered help as part of the overall treatment plan for a family seeking treatment for a parent's alcoholism is both self-identified as the child of an alcoholic and so labeled by the family. The label in this case is a step toward the amelioration of an important family dysfunction. It is presented in the context of interpreting alcoholism as a treatable disease rather than as an immorality or willful misconduct. The labeling process is therefore helpful in the main.

The labeling process may be very different in a program based in an institution to which the child belongs, such as a school, youth group, or camp. A child identified in such a setting runs the risk of being labeled as deviant, at high risk, from "bad seed," or likely to be immoral, neurotic, or psychopathic. These labels may govern the expectations of teachers, academic counselors and peers. They may be translated into choices about leadership roles, academic direction and career guidance. At worst, the labels can represent self-fulfilling prophecies of deviance. Thus, when programs aimed at primary prevention or early intervention for children of alcoholic parents are based in an institution other than a treatment agency, such programs must be structured with great sensitivity and genuine confidentiality.

A school-based program, for example, will require committed backing from the school board, administration, state department of education, parents' association, teachers, and students. This support must be reflected in a policy statement known to and approved by all of these parties, just as an employee assistance program to aid troubled employees requires a strong policy statement agreed to by top management and labor. This statement must (1) recognize alcoholism and drug dependence as diseases requiring treatment; (2) specify that there will be no penalty for participation in the intervention program per se; and (3) guarantee that program records will be kept separate from school records and in the strictest confidentiality allowed by law. Parents will be contacted or information released only under specified conditions and with the consent of the student.

A strong policy statement is merely a step, however, in achieving a climate of acceptance in the school. The program must be explained and discussed in meetings and written materials. It must also become part of the life of the school.

Treatment and Counseling Programs

Parental consent. Treatment agencies are more accustomed to confidentiality policies than school-based programs. However, there are other difficult policy issues that affect treatment services for children of alcoholics. The most important issue for minor children is that parental consent for treatment is required either by statute or common law in most states, up to the age of majority. Exceptions are sometimes made for so-called emancipated minors (those who live independently, those who are married and/or have children), and those undergoing specific treatments (e.g., for venereal disease or early abortion).

The need for parental consent can be a major barrier to the provision of services to children of alcoholics. Even when such a child requests professional assistance, the parents, especially if their own drinking is active, may resent the possible intrusion of others into their family system and may refuse to consent. This situation applies whether the youngster seeks help for his or her own alcohol abuse or for some other physical or emotional problem. In New York State, this barrier was identified as a major problem by the legislative and executive branches, which responded to testimony at a series of public hearings. The problem for policymakers was balancing the rights of the parent and the child. In legislation that became effective in June 1982, voluntary treatment for alcohol abuse or dependence in minors may be provided without parental consent if the following conditions are met:

1. Either the treatment program, recognizing the importance of the family unit, has taken steps to involve the parent(s) or guardian(s) in the treatment but the parent or guardian refuses to consent to treatment which, in the opinion of a physician, is necessary for and in the best interests of the child;

2. Or, in the judgment of a physician, direct contact with the parent or guardian would have a detrimental effect;

3. Treatment is voluntary and under the supervision of a physician;

4. The reasons for providing treatment without parental consent are documented in the record (2).

In 1982, the New York State Division of Alcoholism and Alcohol Abuse promulgated regulations allowing preventive counseling services for children of alcoholic parents under similar conditions. However, a qualified health professional other than a physician is also permitted to approve and provide the counseling (3) These measures have greatly facilitated the provision of services to children of alcoholic parents in New York State and are highly recommended for adoption in other jurisdictions.

Any program providing services for alcohol or drug abuse to the child of an alcoholic parent cannot communicate with the parent without the consent of the child, under federal confidentiality regulations (42, CFR, Part 2). If this consent is not granted, in some jurisdictions, the program may not proceed with treatment. However, where treatment or preventive counseling is allowed without parental consent, as in New York State, the program may find itself in a situation where it can treat the minor, but cannot bill the parents for the child's services.

Insurance coverage and other financing issues. Even when the parents are willing to initiate treatment for their child, health insurance policies often exclude alcoholism services, cover only inpatient services, or provide little help with the cost of family treatment on an outpatient basis. Recent New York legislation mandated outpatient health insurance coverage for the treatment of alcoholism, and directed that up to 20 of 60 visits required as minimum coverage is allowed for visits by family members (4). Health insurance policies across the United States vary widely in their provision of payment for such services at present, and wider coverage would be desirable in many cases.

Programs specifically designated as prevention or treatment resources for children of alcoholics (as distinguished from the treatment of their parents) are often dependent on public funding for their support. O'Gorman gives a brief history of public policy and funding for such programs (5). In the past, the National Institute on Alcohol Abuse and Alcoholism (NIAAA) has played an important role in funding and program demonstration/replication. With the shift in NIAAA's role away from direct service program funding, the states and local governments have played an increasing role. However, the gross inadequacy of public facilities to meet the urgent treatment needs of various groups (e.g., public inebriates, women, youthful offenders, the so-called "working poor," ethnic minorities, and chronically mentally disabled alcoholics) intensifies the competition for scarce resources. Thus programs for children of alcoholics are few in number.

Confidentiality.

Under federal law and regulations (42 CFR, Part 2), the confidentiality of alcohol and drug abuse patient records is carefully protected. Most clinicians support these protections in spite of the fact that they produce extra paperwork (6). Unfortunately, however, the definition of "patient" in the regulations makes it clear that only the records of alcohol or drug abusers are covered. No mention is made of the records of family members. It would be most helpful if such protection were extended to cover programs for children of alcoholics, with the needed adjustment to provide for child abuse reporting as discussed in the next section.

Child Abuse and Neglect—Definitions.

The manner in which each state defines child abuse and neglect can act either as a barrier or an incentive for an alcoholic parent to enter treatment. For example, prior to 1981 in New York State, the use of alcohol or drugs by a parent to the extent of loss of control over the intake of the substance was, by definition, child neglect. Thus if a parent requested help from a public agency for his or her children's temporary care while seeking alcoholism treatment, the parent risked both loss of custody and all the other consequences of being judged a child neglector. This was a real threat and deterrent to treatment, especially for single-parent families of lower socio-economic status. The definition was also a problem for two-parent families in which child custody became an issue in separation or divorce. In such cases, the mere fact that one parent had received treatment for alcoholism labeled that parent as guilty of child neglect, even if recovery had taken place.

Because of these problems, New York State revised its definition in 1981, providing that a parent who is voluntarily participating in a program of rehabilitation will not be automatically considered guilty of neglect on the basis of alcoholism or drug addiction.(7). This policy acts as a treatment incentive rather than as a barrier.

Mandated Treatment for Child-Abusing Parents.

A useful policy for child-abuse or neglect cases in which the parent suffers from alcoholism involves probation with mandated treatment as a sentencing option. Using the model of drinking driver rehabilitation programs, a court could offer the parent the option of an educational program on child abuse and parenting, plus diagnosis and treatment for alcoholism if needed, as an alternative to imprisonment, loss of custody, or other penalty. The probation officer or child protective agency would monitor both the home situation and the progress in recovery. The wish to retain child custody is a powerful motivator from many alcoholic parents.

A more difficult ethical problem is that posed by mandated treatment for the alcoholic woman who is drinking heavily while pregnant. In a recent article on the treatment of problem drinkers in pregnancy, Rosett and colleagues at the Boston City Hospital mentioned that two of the successfully treated women in their group received treatment under court order, with later custody of their unborn child contingent on the attainment of abstinence (8). The policy questions here center around the rights of the mother and those of the fetus, once the prospective mother has decided to carry the pregnancy to term. Such cases will require sophisticated knowledge of teratology and appropriate legislative policy-making in the very near future. What legal responsibility does a pregnant woman owe her fetus? Can she be guilty of prenatal child abuse?

Child-Abuse Reporting by Alcoholism Program Personnel.

There is an unfortunate conflict that arises between two federal laws. One law establishes special confidentiality of alcohol and drug abuse patient records, and another, the Child Abuse Prevention and Treatment Act, encourages states to establish mandatory child-abuse reporting laws. Most states have established such legislation, which requires that teachers, health professionals, and others report suspected cases of child abuse or neglect in their caseloads to state authorities for investigation. If abuse or neglect is found, efforts are made to assist the family, but child custody may be temporarily or permanently lost by the parent, and prosecution is possible. Thus a social worker, for example, treating a 16-year-old alcohol abuser who is being physically or sexually abused by a parent is mandated to report the case. On the other hand, the federal regulations on confidentiality of alcohol or drug abuse records (42 CFR, Part 2) expressly forbid the release of information obtained in an alcoholism or drug abuse program without specific signed consent. In the case of a minor in treatment with parental consent, the parent's signature is also required. Obtaining such consent for child abuse reporting may be difficult. If consent cannot be obtained and the report would necessarily contain material that identifies the subject as someone in treatment for alcohol or drug abuse (for example, if the facility from which the report comes is a clinic which treats only alcohol or drug problems), the treatment provider must obtain a court order to make such a report. Because of the awkwardness of this process, NIAAA and the National Center on Child Abuse and Neglect (NCCAN) issued a joint memorandum in 1978 recommending that alcohol and drug abuse programs negotitate agreements called qualified service organization agreements with the state child abuse reporting agency (9). Under such agreements, information can be provided to the child abuse agency without consent. However, the agreement restricts the receiving agency in how it may use the information, and prohibits redisclosure (for example, to a county child protective agency or a district attorney), making the agreement impractical in some states.

An additional problem is that the initial report is only one of the many stages of an investigation and processing of a child abuse case during which information from a treatment provider would be important (10). The conflict here, again between the rights of child and parent, will probably require a specific policy decision, reflected in new federal legislation, for its ultimate resolution.

Prevention of Fetal Alcohol Syndrome (FAS) and Other Fetal Alcohol Effects(FAE)

FAS, a characteristic syndrome of birth defects found in the children of mothers who drank heavily during pregnancy (usually at the rate of six drinks or more per day for a prolonged period), is thought to be one of the nation's most common causes of mental retardation associated with birth defect. It is found in approximately one to three infants for every 1,000 live births (11). FAE refers to a wider range of birth defects that do not meet the strict diagnostic requirements for FAS but are found in increased incidence in women who use varying amounts of alcohol during pregnancy. Efforts to prevent these two causes of disability are a high public priority. Prevention of FAS and FAE requires four elements: 1. Public education; 2. Professional education; 3. Screening and diagnosis of pregnant woman who have alcohol problems; and 4. Adequate treatment for pregnant problem drinkers and their families. Efforts at prevention of FAS/FAE have brought sharp disagreements about both the content and vehicle for public education messages.

Public Health Recommendations.

In 1981, the U. S. Surgeon General published an advisory warning on alcohol use during pregnancy, and recommending that abstinence from alcohol was the wisest course at the present state of knowledge (12). His position was the same as that of NIAAA, the American Medical Society on Alcoholism, and other groups. On the other hand, educational materials developed and distributed by groups backed by the alcohol beverage industry, such as the Licensed Beverage Information Council, mention only "excessive or abusive drinking" as a hazard (13). This disagreement has been discussed and debated (14,15). Federal public policy will be reflected not only in the Surgeon General's advisory, but in such other federal information sources as the Department of Agriculture's Dietary Guidelines, which are currently undergoing revision. State and local prevention programs will have to develop on their own.

Appropriate Media for Public Health Education about FAS/FAE

If deciding on the proper message for FAS/FAE public education has provoked controversy, arguments over the media by which it ought to be presented have been even more intense. Proposals to require warning labels on beverage alcohol containers or warning posters where such beverages are sold have led to heated disagreement (16). Although the U. S. Senate passed a bill to require warning labels in 1979, the House of Representatives did not. A compromise reached between the two houses called for a federal report on the health hazards of alcohol. This report failed to recommend labeling but called upon the beverage industry to become more involved in public health education (17).

New York City, in 1984, required by law that vendors of alcoholic beverages display a poster that reads "Warning: Drinking alcoholic beverages during pregnancy can cause birth defects." This law was bitterly opposed by the beverage industry in hearings held in 1983. It was also later opposed by certain feminist groups who felt that the warning unfairly singled out women and might subject them to harassment when drinking in public. Other jurisdictions have now passed simliar measures.

Conclusion

There are many important public policy issues that have special relevance to children of alcoholics, only some of which are discussed here. The American public is just now beginning to become aware of this population as a target group for treatment and prevention efforts.

A critical element in U. S. policy has been the support of research in alcoholism, fetal alcohol effects, and other areas relevant to children of alcoholics. Far more resources are needed for all alcohol-related research, which has been chronically underfunded in comparison to research into other health problems (18). Interested scientists attending a conference on Research Needs and Opportunities for Children of Alcoholics, sponsored by the Children of Alcoholics Foundation, have developed an agenda of high priority research needs, and a consensus statement of recommended research policy (19,20).

As awareness grows and knowledge gained through research improves, more and more complex and difficult ethical and policy decisions will be required. Health professionals should be among the leadership in studying, clarifying, and helping to make these decisions so that the best interests of the involved children are neither overlooked nor underserved.

References

1. Freedman, M.K. M.D. points to the family as source of addictive behavior. Letter in *American Medical News*, September 23, 1982.
2. N.Y.S. Division of Alcoholism and Alcohol Abuse, Alcoholism Legislative Review, Albany, New York, 1982.
3. Peters, K.K. Memorandum: Preventative counseling services for children of alcoholics. N. Y. State Division of Alcoholism and Alcohol Abuse, December 6, 1982.
4. N.Y.S. Division of Alcoholism and Alcohol Abuse, Alcoholism Legislative Review, Albany, New York, 1983.
5. O'Gorman, P. Public policy and the child of the alcoholic. *Journal of Children in Contemporary Society.* 1982; 15:35-41.
6. Blume, S.B.. Changing the federal regulations on confidentiality: Views of clinical staff. *Journal on Studies of Alcohol.* 1981;42:344-349.
7. N.Y.S. Division of Alcoholism and Alcohol Abuse, Alcoholism Legislative Review, Albany, New York, 1981.
8. Rosett, H.L., Weiner, L., Edelin, K.C. Treatment experience with pregnant problem drinkers. *Journal of American Medical Association*, 1983;249:2029-2033.
9. Wingspread Conference. Issues in child protection and substance abuse. *Catalyst.* 1980;1:8-13.
10. Wald, D., and Weisberg, J. Confidentiality laws and state efforts to protect abused or neglected children. *Family Law Quarterly.* 1984.
11. U. S. Department of Health and Human Services. Fifth Special Report to the U. S. Congress on Alcohol and Health, USDHHS, Washington, DC, 1983.
12. U.S. Surgeon General Advisory on Alcohol and Pregnancy, *FDA Drug Bulletin.* 1981; 11: 1-2.
13. Robe, L.B. Drinking during pregnancy: Straight talk or double talk? *Alcoholism, The National Magazine.* Sept-Oct, 1982.
14. Kolata, G.B. Fetal alcohol advisory debated. *Science*, 1981; 214:642-645.
15. Blume, S.B. Is social drinking during pregnancy harmless? There is reason to think not. *Advances in Alcohol and Substance Abuse.* 1984.
16. U.S. Senate Committee on Labor and Human Resources, Proceedings of the Subcommittee on Alcoholism and Drug Abuse Hearing on Labeling of Alcoholic Beverages, Sept. 1979.
17. U.S. Dept. of the Treasury and U.S. Dept. of Health and Human Services. Report to the President and Congress on health hazards associated with alcohol and methods to inform the general public of these hazards, Washington. DC 1980.
18. *Institute of Medicine, Alcoholism, Alcohol Abuse and Related Problems: Opportunities for Research.* National Academy Press. Washington, DC 1980.
19. Russell, M., Henderson, C., Blume, S.B. Children of Alcoholics: A Review of the Literature. Children of Alcoholics Foundation, Report of the conference on research needs and opportunities for children of alcoholics. Children of Alcoholics Foundation, New York, 1985.